LOW PAY and How to End It

A UNION VIEW

LOW PAY
and How to End It

A UNION VIEW

Alan Fisher and Bernard Dix

PITMAN PUBLISHING

First published 1974

SIR ISAAC PITMAN AND SONS LTD.
Pitman House, Parker Street, Kingsway, London WC2B 5PB
P.O. Box 46038, Banda Street, Nairobi, Kenya

SIR ISAAC PITMAN (AUST.) PTY. LTD.
Pitman House, 158 Bouverie Street, Carlton, Victoria 3053, Australia

PITMAN PUBLISHING CORPORATION
6 East 43rd Street, New York, N.Y. 10017, U.S.A.

SIR ISAAC PITMAN (CANADA) LTD.
495 Wellington Street West, Toronto 135, Canada

THE COPP CLARK PUBLISHING COMPANY
517 Wellington Street West, Toronto 135, Canada

ISBN: 0 273 00764 5

Text set in 11/13 pt. Monotype Ehrhardt, printed by letterpress,
and bound in Great Britain at The Pitman Press, Bath
G 63:11

Preface

This book has grown out of the practical experiences of those active trade unionists who have been in the forefront of the campaign to eliminate low pay. Without their efforts and inspiration it would never have been written. Our particular thanks are due to the staff of the Research Department of the National Union of Public Employees for the contribution they made to the task of producing this book in a very short period of time and to Alan Anderson of Sheffield Polytechnic for his assistance.

ALAN FISHER
BERNARD DIX

Contents

1. A Case for Commitment

The trouble is not that we ask for too much but that we ask for too little.

TONY BENN

Sooner or later, and it is usually sooner, any discussion on low pay gets bogged down in a problem of definition. The sticking point comes when someone poses the awkward question: Just what do *you* mean by low pay? The answer, like those to most economic, social and political questions, depends very much on the personal circumstances and attitudes of those taking part in the discussion. In recent years, for example, we have seen such diverse groups as business executives, airline pilots, motor car workers, miners and hospital workers arguing—with equal personal conviction—that they are low paid workers. On the surface, with the business executive and airline pilot being paid very much more than the hospital worker, it seems difficult to see how all of these widely differing groups can possibly claim to have low pay as a common complaint. One of the main reasons for this apparent paradox is to be found in the fact that any consideration of low pay leads people to argue from what they think ought to be rather than what actually is. This means that how low pay is defined, and whether or not it exists, depends on personal judgements, values and opinions rather than on any mathematically established formula.

Just how this operates in practice could best be demonstrated if we were able to put to our mixed bag of people who claimed to be low paid the question: In what way do you consider yourself to be low paid? The business executive would point to the fact that Britain was a member of the Common Market and in his day-to-day activities he worked closely with European executives who enjoyed much higher living standards; he might well add that he was making a vital contribution to Britain's export drive and the importance of this was not reflected in his salary cheque. The airline pilot would say that his job had a high responsibility content which made exacting demands on his skills and personal qualities and that pilots of foreign airlines who flew exactly the same routes as he did were paid more. The motor car worker might argue that he was earning less than another car worker doing the same job for a different company which had lower profit than his own firm. The miner would emphasize the conditions under which he worked, illustrating this by the number of miners killed, injured and disabled by industrial disease each year; and he would add that although the coal industry was of increasing strategic importance to the national economy the wages it paid were too low to attract workers. The hospital worker would argue that while his work was of high social value to the community his pay was too low to provide a reasonable standard of living for himself and his family.

Sifting through these answers we can begin to see some of the difficulties involved in defining low pay. First, low pay is a relative concept which can be explained only by reference to something else; very often this reference is to something like high pay or fair pay, terms which themselves cannot be defined in an absolute sense. Second, low pay is a subjective concept; it is assessed at different levels by different people on the basis of widely differing criteria—such as skills, responsibilities, working conditions, the economic or social value of the work performed and living standards. Third, not only do different people assess low pay differently on the basis of differing criteria, but the degree of importance attached to the criteria varies from individual to individual and can shift from time to time to accommodate changing individual circumstances.

It would therefore seem that we are confronted with a confusing, if not impassable, morass in our attempt to define low pay and at this point we could, like some who have trod the path before, throw up our hands in despair with the conclusion that the low paid, like the poor, will always be with us. There is, however, an alternative; this is to develop our own definition of low pay by using our own judgement, values and opinions. In other words, we must present the problem and its solution on the basis of criteria selected and weighted by ourselves. In the process our arguments will inevitably differ from the arguments presented by others who have studied the problem, but it is important to realize that the methods we use to reach our conclusions will be very much the same as those used by them. The real difference is that we must make our values and assumptions explicit because we must not delude ourselves with the belief that it is possible to make any real contribution to the solution of the problems of low pay while claiming to be neutral or dispassionate. We cannot become engaged in an academic exercise, we must grind an axe in the hope that it will be used to good effect.

Therefore, at this early stage, let us make our position quite clear. We are absolutely committed to the belief that low pay is a scandal which can be, and must be, eradicated. We believe that low pay continues to exist in Britain because those who are, and who have been, in a position to do something about it have for too long been constipated by economic and political orthodoxy which—insofar as it is even prepared to admit that a problem of low pay exists—consistently argues that nothing practical or substantial can be done to remove it; an argument which is often used to cloak a conviction that nothing *should* be done to remove it. If we are to force a positive change in this attitude we need political action, which in turn rests on the need to promote organized, informed and articulate action by those who have the potential power to insist that a political solution is applied to the problem of low pay. Those who have this potential are primarily active trade unionists and their allies in the Labour Movement and the axe we are grinding must be used by them.

Because we are convinced that low pay must be solved by political action our examination of low pay must be presented in political terms. In other words, we must approach the problem by emphasizing its social character and substitute collective preferences for individual preferences. If we are to avoid accusations that we are utopian idealists we must also present a policy which is capable of immediate application. On the other hand, we must not compromise essential principles merely to conform to administrative convenience or practicability as defined by those who are not prepared to make the radical changes required to eliminate low pay.

What are the possibilities of support for such an approach, particularly when our earlier examples of the reasons why various groups argued that they were low paid were so divergent as to be incapable of co-ordination or reconciliation?

In our brief examination of those reasons we noted that they were all, in one sense or another, based on relativities. A more careful consideration will show that they tend to fall into two distinct major categories. The first takes as its point of reference the pay of someone else; even arguments about skill or the need to attract labour to a particular industry rest, in the final analysis, on the pay levels of workers in other industries. The second takes as its point of reference the need for a wage high enough to maintain a minimum standard of living, a pay packet sufficient to make ends meet at prevailing price levels. These two categories are, of course, related to one another; but it is the nature of this relationship which marks an important distinction. The first is concerned with establishing a relative standard of living, the second is concerned with meeting basic standards. One is primarily concerned with desires encouraged by prospects of affluence while the other is concerned with needs driven by the fear of poverty.

At this point in time we are convinced that attention must be concentrated on the second category, and that any policy for the elimination of low pay must establish as its foundation a defined level of basic pay sufficient to provide an acceptable basic standard of living. We are further convinced that this level of basic pay must be established through a continuous process of interaction between Government and the trade unions as a legally enforceable national minimum wage; it is this which underlines the political character of our approach.

This is the central principle around which our argument revolves. We are seeking to establish, as a principle on which to continue the discussion, that there should exist some primary level of basic pay below which no worker should fall: a weekly sum which should be in every worker's pay packet as the starting contribution to his total earnings before any account is taken of such factors as overtime, skill, qualifications, bonus payments or anything else. Using this as our central principle we can legitimately ask everybody—be they Cabinet Minister or coal miner, doctor or dustman, film star or factory sweeper—whether they are prepared to accept this principle as one on which a policy for the elimination of low pay can be constructed.

There will be immediate objections. While there will be very few people who will want to be seen giving an outright 'no' as an answer there will be many who will want to respond with a qualified 'yes'.

For example, some higher paid workers—salaried as much as wage earners—will answer: 'Yes, but not if it narrows my own pay differential.'

Some low paid workers will answer: 'Yes, but not if it puts me out of a job.'

Some of their low paying employers will answer: 'Yes, but not if it cuts my profit margins or prices me out of business.'

Some housewives will answer: 'Yes, but not if it puts up the cost of my weekly shopping.'

Some taxpayers will answer: 'Yes, but not if I have to pay more income tax.'

Some politicians will answer: 'Yes, but not if it puts up export prices, upsets the balance of payments and sinks the pound.'

And most shareholders will answer: 'Yes, but not if it cuts my dividends.'

These qualifications are legitimate, but they belong to a later stage of the discussion. What we are seeking to do at this point is to use an accepted method of analysis and enquiry by introducing the central theoretical principle which we intend to use as the basis of our case for eliminating low pay. We know that in politics, probably more than anywhere else, theoretical principles are so often surrounded by practical problems as to make them seem inoperable. But we also know from personal experience that in politics those people who reject a principle often surround their rejection with a smokescreen of apparent practical problems because they want to make that principle inoperable without having to stand up and oppose that principle in full view of the voting public.

For our part, we are convinced that the first step in the construction of a policy to eliminate low pay must be the acceptance of the principle that there is a level of wages below which nobody should be expected to work. This is an act of political commitment which has been dodged in most of the earlier discussions on low pay but which is essential if the problems of the low paid worker are to become a matter demanding an immediate practical solution rather than remaining the subject of a detached academic curiosity. With public acceptance of this principle we can begin to fill out the arguments and examine the problems which confront us in the implementation of the principle in the full knowledge that we are committed to action rather than never-ending discussion.

2. The Affluent Society

> The main effect of classical wage theories has been to justify an existing situation by explaining an imaginary one.
>
> BARBARA WOOTTON

Looking back it is difficult to believe that throughout the latter part of the 1950s, when the immediate period of post-war readjustment had passed, Britain could exist in a state of euphoria which showed scant concern for the many families who were by no means convinced that the affluent society—delivered in giant size economy packets by optimistic politicians and sycophantic mass media—had at last arrived. While Super Mac, the cartoon caricature who became political reality, managed to convince not only himself but most of the population that they had never had it so good, the sore of low pay was festering.

One of the major difficulties facing those who were at that time attempting to direct attention to the problem of low pay in the allegedly affluent society was the inadequacy of reliable statistics from official sources. For some twenty years those engaged in the process of wage negotiation, and those commenting on the process, had taken as their primary source of comparative earnings the results of the half-yearly surveys conducted each April and October by what was then the Ministry of Labour. These results, published in the *Ministry of Labour Gazette*, showed the average weekly earnings (including all overtime, piecework, bonus and other payments but before deductions for tax and National Insurance) of 'manual workers employed in the manufacturing industries generally and in a number of the principal non-manufacturing industries in the United Kingdom.'

The surveys were deficient in a number of respects. For example, because they excluded non-manual workers and because they did not include all industries and services they gave less than total coverage of the workforce as a whole. Much more important, however, their results were presented as a crude national average and equally crude averages for the 128 industrial groups covered by the survey. Because this made it possible for workers to get some very rough indication of how the average earnings in their industrial groups compared with the national average and with the averages of the other industrial groups this comparison was often used as a measure of high pay or low pay. In fact the survey results, as is often the case with inadequate statistics, concealed more than they revealed. To gain any real information on the extent of low pay it was necessary to probe behind the industry-wide averages and to show a distribution of earnings which would establish the number or proportion of workers falling within particular ranges of earnings. It was precisely this information which the half-yearly survey failed to present.

A breakthrough came in October 1960 when the Ministry of Labour responded, in its own words, to 'a growing demand from many quarters and for many purposes', and collected information on the distribution of manual workers' earnings in addition to its normal half-yearly survey. The results, published in the *Ministry of Labour Gazette* in April and June of the following year, were primitive by today's standards; but they provided a statistical foundation on which a case for action against low pay could be constructed and which should have disturbed the complacency of those who were still basking in the artificial sunshine of the affluent society.

On the basis of the results of the old half-yearly survey in October 1960 the overall average weekly earnings of full-time male manual workers aged 21 and over were £14·53. The new figures on the distribution of earnings made it possible, for the first time, to compare what proportion of these workers earned less than the average and how much less they earned. An extract from the main results is shown in Table 2.1, and it makes depressing reading. It shows, for example, that nearly three workers in every ten earned less than £12 a week while one in every ten earned less than £10 a week—or little more than two-thirds of the national average.

Table 2.1. Distribution of weekly earnings, full-time male manual workers, October 1960[1]

Percentage with weekly earnings less than													
£8	£10	£12	£14	£16	£18	£20	£22	£24	£26	£28	£30	£40	£50
0·98	9·99	27·90	48·40	66·45	79·59	99·28	93·56	96·56	98·20	99·02	99·44	99·94	99·99

For a nation in which politicians were devoting most of their attention to how to cope with the imagined problems of new-found prosperity, these statistics should have had the effect of a cold shower. For those trade union negotiators who were satisfied merely because the half-yearly surveys had shown their industrial group above the national average, the detailed break-down of the distribution of earnings should have caused serious thoughts on their future wage bargaining strategy. The distribution of earnings survey, using what are described as the Minimum List Headings of the main 128 industrial groups, not only confirmed the concentration of low pay in particular industries, it also showed that in many industries which were not regarded as low paid by average earnings standards there were significant pockets of low paid workers.

Local government manual workers, for example, were widely recognized as low paid; with average earnings of £10·80 in October 1960 they were £3·73 below the national average figure. The distribution of earnings survey not only confirmed this situation, it also showed just how black it was. More than 93 per cent of these workers earned below the national average and nearly 60 per cent of them earned less than the miserably low average of £10·80 of local government manual workers. Right at the bottom of the scale, 42 per cent earned less than £10 per week: in other words, the proportion of local government manual workers below the £10 level was more than four times the national figure. In this way the earnings distribution survey clearly demonstrated that local government was not only low paid overall but that it contained very large concentrations of low paid workers.

At the other end of the spectrum, some of the industries which had rather smugly assumed that the workers in them were not particularly troubled by problem of low pay—because the industries' average earnings figures were above the national average—were shown to have groups of workers who had legitimate cause for complaint. In the engineering industry overall, for example, the average earnings were £15·25 or £0·72 above the national average; but the earnings distribution survey showed that more than 16 per cent of the men producing agricultural machinery and more than 18 per cent of those in ordnance factories were below the £10 earnings level. Even in the printing and publishing of newspapers and periodicals, where the average earnings of £18·84 were the highest recorded in the half-yearly survey and £4·31 above the national average, more than a fifth of the men had earnings below average and 7·5 per cent were below £12 a week.

The significance of these results was underlined when the Ministry of Labour, in a further analysis, showed the distribution of earnings using a different statistical method based on the median value.

The median value is the middle amount in an earnings scale; thus one half of the workers covered have earnings above this amount and one half have earnings below. To show the spread of earnings, other values are taken above and below the median.

The lower quartile is the amount in earnings which marks the boundary between the lowest paid quarter and the highest paid three quarters; thus one quarter have earnings below this amount and three quarters have earnings above.

The highest decile is the amount which marks the boundary of the highest paid tenth; thus one tenth have earnings above this amount and the remainder below.

When earnings statistics are presented in this fashion a worker is able to make a number of comparisons which tell him a great deal about his position relative to other workers in his own industry, to workers in other industries and to workers as a whole. Thus a worker who is low paid relative to his own industry is able to compare his position with those who are the lowest paid in other industries and those who are low paid relative to the workforce in total. The results of the 1960 distribution of earnings survey, presented in this fashion, thus illuminated the problem of low pay which then existed. Table 2.2 gives an example of the kind of information provided by taking all the industries covered, the industry with the highest median (newspaper and periodical printing) and the industry with the lowest median (local government).

Table 2.2 Distribution of weekly earnings (medians, quartiles and deciles), male manual workers, October 1960[2]

	Lowest Decile	*Lower Quartile*	*Median*	*Upper Quartile*	*Highest Decile*
All industries covered	£10·00	£11·71	£14·17	£17·24	£20·58
Local government	£9·00	£9·48	£10·39	£11·81	£13·68
Printing, Publishing of Newspapers and Periodicals	£12·44	£14·68	£18·41	£23·96	£30·44

The conclusions that can be drawn from these figures are many and self evident. For example, in the lowest paid industry (local government) the highest decile was £0·48 below the median for all industries and even in the highest paid industry (printing) the lowest decile was £1·73 below the all industries median. In other words, although the median for the printing industry was £8·02 above that for local government there were still workers in the printing industry who could correctly be described as low paid, not only in relation to their own industry but in relation to the median for all industries.

Surprisingly enough, the significance of these findings in the 1960 distribution of earnings survey attracted little attention at the time and did little to promote political pressure on the low pay issue. And, despite the paucity of statistical material, the survey remained the only official excursion into this crucial area for nearly a decade to come. The next development of note came from independent sources, and that not until 1967 when two academics—Derek Robinson and Judith Marquand—simultaneously published articles on low pay. Robinson was prompted by the attempts to construct an incomes policy and Marquand by other studies into the problems of family poverty. In a sense, however, both were concerned with the need to identify the low paid worker, whose existence had by then been recognized but who so far had not been accurately described, either by the Government or any of its agencies. In the absence of more recent material, both based their work on the 1960 distribution of earnings survey which we have previously considered.

Robinson,[3] on the assumption that the distribution of earnings had remained relatively stable over the period, used the results of the continuing half-yearly survey of average earnings to update the findings of the 1960 distribution of earnings survey. On this basis he was able to estimate the distribution of earnings for the 128 industrial groups in October 1966. As an example, Table 2.3 shows his estimated percentage of men earning less than given amounts in all the industries covered and in local government.

Table 2.3. Estimated distribution of weekly earnings, male manual workers, October 1966

	Percentage with weekly earnings less than					
	£10	£11	£12	£13	£14	£15
All industries covered	0·51	0·91	2·53	5·55	10·16	15·91
Local government	0·57	1·33	4·14	9·67	31·36	49·40

Similarly, Table 2.4 shows his estimated lowest decile and lower quartile values for all industries and for local government.

Insofar as it is ever possible to separate the two when discussing low pay, Robinson's paper was a technical exercise rather than a political one. He presented the available data in several different ways while specifically refraining from choosing from them '. . . an arbitrary level below which workers are considered to be low paid.' In this he was fulfilling what is considered to be the classic role of an economic adviser; by remedying deficiencies in official statistics he was presenting his own findings for others to draw any necessary political conclusions. Anticipating possible questions, Robinson wrote, '. . . it might be asked whether these figures are of any value at all. The answer is that there are no others.' The fact that Robinson felt it necessary to make such a comment is an indication that, as late as 1967, the growing discussion on low pay was still largely unsupported by any real up-to-date information.

Marquand[4] also used the 1960 distribution of earnings survey as a starting point and added to it some industries not included in that original survey. On this basis she sought to identify '. . . the main groups of low paid male workers whose pay may be too low to

Table 2.4. Estimated lower decile and quartile values, weekly earnings of male manual workers, October 1966

	Lowest Decile	*Lower Quartile*
All industries covered	£13·97	£16·37
Local government	£13·04	£13·73

maintain an adequate standard of living', and she offered two alternative—and in some cases complementary—standards by which low pay might be identified for the purpose of analysis. The first suggested that those industries falling into the lowest quartile when the 128 industrial groups were ranked according to the earnings levels of workers in the lowest decile might be considered as low paid industries. The second hinged upon workers' individual pay levels rather than on general industry-related comparisons. It suggested that low paid industries might be defined as those with more than 2,000 employees earning less than £9 a week and/or those with more than 5,000 employees earning less than £10 a week in October 1960 (unlike Robinson, Marquand did not attempt to update the 1960 distribution of earnings survey).

Her first definition produced a list of 32 industrial groups, 15 of which were covered by Wages Councils, in which the lowest decile earnings ranged from £8·20 to £9·46. Marquand's second method produced a list of 21 industrial groups of which eight also appeared in her first list and were therefore covered by both of her suggested definitions of low pay. The remaining 13 in the second list, although not revealed in her earlier approach as low paid industries, were shown in fact to employ large numbers of workers at low earnings levels.

Like Robinson, Marquand was primarily concerned with presenting the evidence which showed the existence of low paid workers, and in the process to demonstrate the need for adequate and up-to-date statistical information on earnings distribution. She did, however, show a greater tendency towards suggesting standards by which low pay should be judged. It is perhaps convenient at this point, therefore, to consider briefly some of the current definitions of low pay which are used in contemporary arguments because these originated, at least in part, with writers like Robinson and Marquand in the period we have been considering.

We have, for example, the definition which says that a worker is low paid if his earnings fall below the lowest decile value for all industries. We have the definition which says a worker is low paid if his earnings fall below a fixed proportion, usually two-thirds, of the all industry median. And we have the definition which takes a fixed weekly minimum sum expressed in monetary terms.

All of these definitions have their origins, at least in part, in the discussions on low pay which were taking place amongst academics in the latter half of the 1960s. There is one further definition, however, which—although Marquand hinted at it—we have not yet seen emerge. This is the definition which relates low pay to the official 'poverty level' as defined by Government through its payments of social security benefits. This definition owes its origins not so much to specific research into low pay as such but to an examination of the much wider general problem of poverty, and to low pay as just one of the factors contributing to poverty.

The pioneering work in this area was carried out by Brian Abel-Smith and Peter Townsend between 1961 and 1963 and their findings were published in 1965. Using statistics published by the Ministry of Labour in its regular Family Expenditure Surveys, Abel-Smith and Townsend set out to establish the comparative extent of poverty in Britain at two points in time, 1953–54 and 1960. As with studies of low pay, studies of poverty meet with the initial problem of definition and to overcome this Abel-Smith and Townsend—rather than apply their own personal value judgements —accepted the 'official' definition: the minimum living standards as operated by the then National Assistance Board.

Their findings[5] were nothing less than startling. They showed that in 1953–54 more than 600,000 people (or 1·2 per cent of the population) were living below the basic National Assistance level plus a rent allowance and were thus in 'primary poverty'. A further 3,300,000 (6·6 per cent of the population) were living at 40 per cent above this level and were therefore in 'secondary poverty'. Of particular significance was the fact that of these 4 million people living in poverty more than a third of them were in households whose head was in full-time work.

If these figures for 1953–54 were startling, those for 1960 were nothing less than shocking, for they revealed that the problems of poverty—far from diminishing with the arrival of the affluent society—were actually increasing. By 1960 the number of people living in primary poverty had risen to almost 2 million (3·8 per cent of the population) while those living in secondary poverty had risen to almost 5 million (10·4 per cent). Within this overall picture, the low pay factor continued to play a significant part: more than 3 million people living in poverty were in households dependent on earnings or 'other private income'; in other words, four out of every ten people living in primary or secondary poverty were in this position.

This work by Abel-Smith and Townsend demonstrated quite clearly, even by the Government's own definition of minimum acceptable living standards on the not over–generous norms of the National Assistance Board, that widespread poverty existed and that low pay was an important cause of that poverty.

Official confirmation of this independent research came soon afterwards in two reports from the Ministry of Social Security, as it had become, in 1967. The first[6] reported the results of an enquiry in mid-1966 into the circumstances of families with two or more children who were receiving family allowances. The report showed that of the 3·9 million families in this category there were 280,000 (7·1 per cent) whose resources were below National Assistance scales and that in a quarter of these the father was in full-time work. When measured against the levels of then recently introduced Supplementary Benefit scales—which were marginally higher—the report disclosed an even more serious situation with 345,000 families, containing well over a million children, below these levels. Once again the effect of low pay was shown by the fact that in more than one-third of these cases the father was in full-time work. Even this report, however, understated the extent to which low pay was a factor of poverty because it did not encompass families with less than two children. This gap was filled to some extent by the second report[7] which estimated that there were probably a further 15,000 families with less than two children whose father was in full-time work with earnings below the Supplementary Benefit level. On the basis of these two reports, then, there were 140,000 families with a weekly income below Supplementary Benefit levels, despite the fact that the father was in full-time employment.

It is true, of course, that depending on the methods used and the standards adopted, there were discrepancies between the various estimates of people who might be considered low paid in the 1960s on the basis of the studies we have looked at, but at this distance in time those discrepancies are not important. What is important is to realise that, even after making allowances for inadequate statistical information, it was possible for those who were interested to pose some serious and sensible questions about low pay. As a result, it was possible to demonstrate that low paid workers existed and that low pay was a major contributory factor in family poverty.

Low pay therefore ceased to be a technical exercise and became —or should have become—a political question. No longer was it necessary to ask: Are there low paid workers? Instead the relevant questions became, or should have become: How many people are low paid and by what standards? and, the crunch question: What are we going to do about it? These are crucial political questions and the way in which they were answered, or even considered, depended very much on value judgements. We must now see how the major interest groups tackled them.

3. An Opportunity Missed

> There is no doubt that the overlooking of particular groups of low paid people was the first cause of the break-out from incomes policy.
>
> ALEX A. JARRATT

During the early part of the 1960s the trade union Movement in total, as identified by the TUC, gave little or no attention to the problems of low pay as such. Instead it was preoccupied with debate, both internal and with the Tory Government, on the wider issue of general wage restraint. The Government, transfixed by its desire to reconcile the apparent contradictions between maximum economic growth and strains on the balance of payments, had opted for policies which placed their main emphasis on the limitation of wage increases. As a consequence the attention of the TUC was directed towards constructing a policy which, while rejecting Government imposed wage restraint, was designed to protect living standards by minimizing the dangers of either unemployment or inflation. With hindsight it can be argued that in the process the TUC, and its affiliated unions, allowed the Government to deflect their attention from the specific problem of low pay which—had it been pursued—could have demonstrated the inadequacies of an inflexible and arbitrary policy of governmental wage restraint.

An example of this missed opportunity can be illustrated by the major economic debate at the 1963 Trades Union Congress, when the General Council presented a lengthy and detailed policy document, entitled *Economic Development and Planning*,[1] in which it justified its decision to participate in the work of the National Economic Development Council and asserted that unions must accept the fact that the NEDC would inevitably become involved in matters directly relating to wages. Low pay was not specifically mentioned in the document which, almost as an aside, posed the questions: 'Can collective bargaining machinery be used to secure a more just and equitable distribution of personal income, which would involve trade unionists in taking account of the effects of their actions on fellow trade unionists in other industries? To what extent and how can trade unionists influence such national objectives as ... the redistribution of the nation's wealth?' As if in self answer the document added: 'Any agreement, within the framework of economic planning, on a wages strategy which involved unions in modifying their own bargaining objectives could only be reached within the context of more general agreement on national economic and social priorities.' During the debate on the document at the Congress—in which 18 well-established union leaders participated, including eight members of the General Council—the major attention was directed to wage restraint, and the questions posed in the General Council's document remained unanswered. The only direct reference to low pay during the debate came from Ron Smith, then General Secretary of the Union of Post Office Workers, when he said: '... there has got to be recognition of the service industry, of the unskilled worker, of the lower paid people—nearly two million of them still earning only £10 a week and less in this country. We have got to do something in their interests as well as in those of the other sections of the community.'

A month later the main economic debate at the Annual Conference of the Labour Party[2] again demonstrated the preoccupation of both the trade unions and the Labour Party with the overall problem of wage restraint and incomes policy to the exclusion of any specific consideration of the problem of low pay. The conference was dominated by a major speech by Harold Wilson when he introduced a policy document *Labour and the Scientific Revolution.* Taking its cue from the success of the promotion of the affluent society by the Tory Party, the document posed as the central issue of politics how the new riches should be distributed, how the new powers now released by science should be controlled, how full employment should be secured and how the leisure made possible by science should be used. The optimism generated by Harold Wilson's speech washed over the debate on economic affairs. For example, Jack Cooper, then General Secretary of the General and Municipal Workers' Union, argued the need for an incomes policy within the framework of an economic plan by saying: 'If we are to plan for expansion and fail to plan for distribution, not only can gross inequalities develop but our economic advance can be undermined by inflation.' Frank Cousins, then General Secretary of the Transport & General Workers' Union, introduced what was to become a much over-worked phrase, 'the planned growth of incomes' and said: 'We mean we want a planned economic rate of growth which will enable us to have improvements in our real standards of wages.' Summing up on behalf of the Party's National Executive, James Callaghan said: 'The framework in which we shall try to work out an incomes policy is: first, there must be an expanding economy; secondly, the Government's policy must work in harmony with the policies we are asking the trade unions and the employers to follow. For example, that we should not push up prices by our own policies, that we should curb the racketeers and the rent speculators and the rest of them, and that we should act on monopolies.'

Thus, when the crucial formative debates on incomes and wages were taking place within the trade union and Labour Movement in 1963 there was little recognition of the vital need to build into the general policies a specific element designed to solve the particular problem of the low paid section of the working class. Instead there was a general acceptance that the entire problem was to manage the economic policy of a society in the stage of scientific revolution in such a way that it would maximize the employment of productive resources and that wages would increase in proportion to rising productivity while unemployment was eliminated and prices stabilized. In this way the resulting 'planned growth of incomes' would produce a corresponding rise in living standards including, presumably, those of the low paid.

It would be easy, perhaps too easy, to blame the trade union and

Labour Movement for its failure to appreciate the problems of the low paid worker and how the construction of policies to meet these problems would have added a missing social dimension to its general economic policies. The initial blame, however, must rest with the Conservative Government and its allies. With their political advertising campaign to sell the affluent society they had created a market for the product and in the process had blunted the sensibilities of the country to the fact that there were many workers who were too low paid to qualify for entry into that market. The failure of the trade union and Labour Movement, particularly the Labour Party, in this period was that it attempted to meet the Tories on their own terms when it should have concentrated more of its energies on exposing the reality of the low paid worker behind the facade of the affluent society. When the Labour Party took power in 1964 its policies as Government reflected this failure.

Within two months of taking office in October 1964 the Labour Government, the TUC and the employers' organizations produced their famous *Joint Statement of Intent on Productivity, Prices and Incomes*, which displayed the same lack of awareness of the need to promote positive policies to eliminate low pay as had the earlier debates within the trade union and Labour Movement. Insofar as it contained any reference to low pay, the statement was oblique and vague and was in one phrase which said that the social objective of the Government was 'to ensure that the benefits of faster growth are distributed in a way that satisfied the claims of social need and justice.' Four months later, in its first White Paper on prices and incomes policy, the Government was slightly more explicit when laying down the criteria to be followed by the National Board for Prices and Incomes (NBPI) which it had set up to administer its policy. After laying down a norm of approximately 3–3½ per cent for the average rate of annual increase in wages and salaries, the White Paper recognized that increases above this norm would be necessary in some exceptional cases; but added these should be kept to a minimum and would need to be balanced by lower than average increases to other groups. One of the exceptional circumstances—there were four in total—in which increases above the norm could be considered was, 'where there is general recognition that existing wage and salary levels are too low to maintain a reasonable standard of living.'

Both the Joint Statement and the White Paper were included in a report which the TUC General Council presented to a conference of Executive Committees[3] of affiliated unions at the end of April and which was addressed by George Brown, then the Secretary of State for Economic Affairs. Despite the fact that four months earlier he had heralded the Joint Statement as marking the end of the class war, George Brown made no attempt at that conference to explain how the Government intended to meet the claims of social need and justice in relation to the low paid. Nor did he attempt to define what the White Paper meant when it talked about wages and salaries that were too low to maintain a reasonable standard of living. His only passing recognition that there were low paid workers came when he argued that a 'free-for-all' in collective bargaining would not redistribute wealth but would push up prices, wreck the economy and punish what he called the 'weaker members of society.' He sought to underline his argument by adding: 'Those with the strongest bargaining power are not necessarily those with the greatest need.'

Even at this early stage, the shortcomings in the Labour Government's policy were recognized by some trade unions, particularly those representing low paid workers. For example, only a month after George Brown had addressed the TUC conference of executives the Executive Council of the National Union of Public Employees presented a report to its National Conference[4] which spelled out the dangers inherent in the Government's incomes policy: 'It is widely believed that the primary purpose of an incomes policy is to stabilize prices, profits and wages and other forms of income in relation to the overall growth in national production. This concept, however, can be dangerous oversimplification if it leads to an acceptance of the present division of national wealth. We are convinced that an incomes policy based on social and economic justice must assist in breaking down the present class structure of society by redistributing the nation's wealth in favour of the working class. For members of NUPE such a policy involves consistent and deliberate measures designed to secure a substantial increase in the earnings of public employees in order to narrow the existing earnings differential between public employees and workers in manufacturing industries.'

These views were reinforced in the major resolution on wages passed by the NUPE conference which said, in part: 'Recognizing that any national incomes policy based on a fixed percentage growth rate will increase the gap between the highest and the lowest paid workers, Conference urges the Executive Council to impress upon the TUC the need for a policy which will give priority to the needs of lower paid workers.'

The main emphasis in the trade union Movement, however, was still concentrated on the wider problem of wage restraint; and this emphasis was strengthened by the Government's decision, in the autumn of 1965, to enact legislation which would require the notification of all wage claims and prospective terms of settlements to the NBPI and for pay increases to be deferred until the NBPI had reported on them. Many unions saw this as the first breach in the voluntary character of the incomes policy and it was this theme which dominated the economic debate at the 1965 Trades Union Congress.[5] It is true that, as part of the debate, a resolution was proposed which expressed 'grave concern over the economic position of the lower paid workers'; and to support this resolution John Vickers, General Secretary of the Civil Service Union, produced wage slips which he said showed that the take home pay of one of his members—a government messenger in a big provincial city—had risen by a total of 2½p, to just over £9, in the two year period from May 1963 to May 1965. It is equally true that the resolution was passed without opposition; but with the leaders of most major unions—and the TUC General Council—concentrating their energies to defend or attack the latest development in Government incomes policy this resolution on low pay sank almost without trace.

Ironically, it was yet a further tightening of the Government's incomes policy which opened the way for the trade union Movement to begin to focus its attention on the need to develop a policy specifically designed to meet the needs of the low paid. In July 1966 the Prime Minister, Harold Wilson, told the House of Commons that because money incomes had been increasing at a rate far faster than could be justified by increasing production the Government proposed to introduce measures which would impose a standstill on incomes and prices for six months. This period of standstill would be followed by a further period of six months of 'severe restraint.' Following lengthy discussion with the Government the TUC General Council 'reluctantly acquiesced' in the proposal for a standstill; in its detailed report to the 1966 Congress,[6] the General Council attempted to justify this course of action, saying in the process that it believed that the operation of the Government's policy 'must take account of the need to promote social equity, in particular to protect groups of very low paid workers.'

Once again the major emphasis during the Congress debate was on the wider general issue of wage restraint, but this time there was a significant difference. In addition to the General Council's report, the Congress also had before it a resolution which—while pledging support for the Labour Government's prices and incomes policy 'on the basis of similar treatment to all incomes, prices and dividends with the objective of raising the living standards of our people'—demanded 'effective measures to assist lower paid workers, particularly those whose earnings are close to modern conceptions of subsistence levels.' To support this demand, the resolution asked the General Council to investigate ways and means by which the White Paper criteria on exceptional increases for the low paid could be made effective. This resolution introduced a new element into the discussion and, despite the easy assumption by the General Council that those unions which supported the resolution would automatically support the General Council's report and its reluctant acquiescence in wage standstill, the debate demonstrated that some unions had begun to develop more sophisticated attitudes.

In speaking to the resolution, Lord Cooper—then General Secretary of the General and Municipal Workers' Union, one of the major sponsors of the resolution—said that there were three stages in the problem of lower paid workers: to define them, to locate them and to decide how to help them. He suggested that workers earning £12 to £13 a week or less should be given first priority, and admitted that this was pitching the level 'very very low indeed'. On statistical evidence he said that there were probably more than 600,000 male workers in this category and that they were to be found in every industry but with the largest concentrations in the public sector; he added that these figures were based on an up-dating of the 1960 Ministry of Labour survey of the distribution of earnings and emphasized the need for another survey of that kind. When it came to deciding how to assist the low paid, Lord Cooper was less specific. 'Unless it is accepted that the problem should be dealt with by a national minimum wage, which must be at least considered as a possibility, the primary responsibility for securing preferential treatment for low paid workers in private industry must rest on the trade unions themselves. The Government or the Prices and Incomes Board must state what is desirable for low paid workers but the power to do something about it resides in the trade union sides of negotiating bodies and at the bargaining table.'

Despite this very effective support for the low paid the G & MWU, as was made clear by a subsequent speaker from that union, had also decided to support the General Council's report and its 'reluctant acquiescence' in the wage standstill. Other unions took a different stance, and this was demonstrated by NUPE which had decided to support the resolution because it specifically related to low pay but to oppose prevailing Government policy by voting against the General Council's report. Alan Fisher, then Assistant General Secretary of NUPE, explained to the Congress why the Union had taken this position. The General Council, he said, had argued that the operation of the Government's policy must promote social equity and protect lower paid workers but so far as NUPE was concerned this condition had not been met. 'This Friday', he told the delegates, 'a quarter of a million men in local government, whose earnings are £4 10s. a week below the national average, would have had a rise of 11s. a week in their pay packets. It will not be there; it is frozen . . . What the General Council and the Government should have done, if they wanted the full support of the unions, was to have built a minimum wage into their policy so that we all know what is really meant when we talk about lower paid workers.' When the votes were counted at the end of the debate there were clearly many other unions like NUPE who supported the resolution because of its concern for the low paid and then negated the earlier section of the resolution (which pledged support for the Labour Government's incomes policy) by voting against the General Council's report. While the resolution was carried by a comfortable majority of 1,122,000 votes the General Council's report barely scraped through with a majority of 344,000. The message, quite clearly, was that a significant section of the trade union Movement was determined that measures to combat low pay must be an integral part of any incomes policy if it was to be acceptable to trade unionists.

The effect of this change of attitude rapidly became apparent. Immediately after the Congress the TUC General Council undertook a comprehensive review of future incomes policy in relation to overall economic planning. In November 1966, just two months after the Congress, the General Council issued a detailed statement[7] in which it said: 'It is the context in which it is put forward, the objectives it embodies, and the form which it takes which will determine whether an incomes policy is accepted by trade unionists.' The statement concluded with an unmistakable exposition of the considerations which would shape trade union attitudes on incomes policy, and in the process demonstrated that low pay was now a definite item on the agenda:

'Trade unionists are not interested in an incomes policy which is based on the assumption that the share of the national income going to working people will remain the same. The interest lies in a radical and progressive incomes policy which will increase their share in the nation's wealth. Nor do the General Council accept it as axiomatic that, if some working people get more than some predetermined norm, it follows automatically that other working people must get less. What trade unionists are concerned about—and Congress has repeatedly made this clear—is that the standards of some people should be pushed forward faster than those of others. The people who should be pushed forward fastest of all are those who by common consent are in the ranks of the low-paid. Those who should be held back are mainly to be found in the ranks of the top ten per cent of the population who receive at least twenty-five per cent (and almost certainly a good deal more) of the nation's income including all non-wage incomes. These people have not been notably affected by incomes policy as it has operated so far. It is for the Government to identify these people, about whom there is much less information available than about wage earners, and to take action which will convince working people that incomes policy has not only an economic purpose but a social justification.'

Unfortunately this significant development in the trade union approach to incomes policy was not reciprocated by the Government. Almost coincidental with the TUC General Council's statement the Government, in November 1966, issued a White Paper[8] which set out the criteria for wage increases during the period of severe restraint to follow the wages standstill. It contained no new proposals for dealing with low pay specifically; but in a section entitled 'Lowest Paid' it set out what was to become the Government attitude towards low pay for the next eighteen months:

'Improvement of the standard of living of the worst-off members of the community is primarily a social objective. As in practice the needs of individual workers are largely determined by the extent of their family commitments, the Government will continue to give a high priority to measures specifically designed to meet family needs. However, it will be necessary to ensure that any pay increases justified on this ground are genuinely confined to the lowest paid workers and not passed on to other workers. It will be necessary to take into account both earnings and hours worked.'

As a statement of Government policy, and as a guideline for the NBPI in administering that policy, the White Paper was a remarkably confusing document. It established 'family need' as a criterion without attempting to define it in quantitative terms; it confined itself to the 'lowest paid' without recognizing that it was possible to be above that level and still be low paid; it implied that the problem was one to be dealt with by Government fiscal and social security policies rather than by action on employers through the wage packet; and by including the reference to 'earnings and hours' it skated over the problem of low basic wage rates. Subsequent reports of the NBPI reflected this confusion.

In March 1967, for example, the NBPI in Report 29[9] reached the conclusion that local authorities' services and the National Health

Service contained 'large concentrations of workers whose earnings are amongst the lowest in the country'. The report said that the close relationship between earnings for a normal working week and standard wage rates made it impossible to recommend a solution where pay increases were related to different earnings levels. Nor, said the report, was it possible to confine increases to particular wage rates because the wage rate structures were so compressed that to increase wage rates at the bottom grades 'to an extent that would provide meaningful assistance to the lowest paid' would swamp many differentials.

'The corollary is that assistance to the low paid can be given only through a general increase in wage rates. But if all workers in either industry were paid substantially more for the work now performed by the methods now in use, this would impose an unreasonable burden on the ratepayer and the taxpayer and be incompatible with the requirements of prices and incomes policy. Therefore any solution along these lines must be ruled out. There is therefore no immediate answer to the problem of low pay in these services.'

From this approach the NBPI concluded that the 'root cause' of low pay in local authorities' services and the National Health Service was low productivity and any remedy would need to be a long-term policy to tackle both matters by directly relating pay to improvements in efficiency and productivity.

Without arguing against the need to improve the efficiency of the local government and health services, nor to deny that this could help to improve earnings levels, the notable failure of the NBPI's approach in this report—which was repeated in others—was its refusal to consider any solution to the problem of low pay which was not related to improved productivity. Given the confusing guidelines set out by the Government in its White Paper, this approach was inevitable because it was politically safe. It was an approach which five years later led Allan Fels, in an independent study commissioned by the NBPI,[10] to comment 'The NBPI, and the prices and incomes policies, both accorded a lower priority to low pay than to other wage problems, and up to a point tried to subsume the problem into that of raising productivity . . . the NBPI was less vociferous about low pay as a social and economic problem than about other wage problems. This illustrates the general theme which applies to nearly all of the NBPI's work. It did not regard the alteration of the existing distribution of income as one of the main purposes of incomes policy, unless greater efficiency or wage stability was likely to result.'

For their part, the trade unions had embarked on a different course of action. Following a TUC conference of executive committees in March 1967, at which the General Council had received an overwhelming vote in favour of the development of an incomes policy in which the trade union Movement itself decided orders of priority, the General Council's Incomes Policy Committee had been paying detailed attention to the problem of low pay. The report[11] of the General Council to the annual Congress in September 1967 presented tangible evidence of the considerations thrown up by this new activity.

One of the more difficult problems in defining low pay, said the General Council's report, was whether the definition should be based on wage rates or earnings. In many cases, rates bore little relation to earnings and if used by themselves were likely to produce a distorted picture. On the other hand, a figure for average earnings concealed more than it revealed—particularly where the difference between rates and earnings was entirely or mainly due to overtime. The report therefore concluded that the most appropriate method of assisting low paid workers was to aim at progressively raising national minimum rates to a level of £15 a week but to try to concentrate the resulting improvements on workers whose earnings (exclusive of overtime) were at or near the minimum rate. In establishing this as a priority, the General Council said that the decision 'to discriminate directly in favour of low paid workers would not mean that the claims of better paid workers would be ignored but rather that they would need to be justified by reference to other considerations, and mainly by reference to improvements in productivity.'

At the Congress itself this dual approach was underwritten in a resolution moved by the Transport and General Workers' Union General Secretary Frank Cousins, which expressed opposition to restrictive and negative incomes policies and called for a high wage–

high efficiency policy; directed 'special attention' to the problem of the lower paid and called for a minimum wage of £15 a week ('or its annual equivalent on current living costs') for a normal 40 hour week or less; and urged the General Council to give considerations to the need for up-to-date statistics for the development of a co-ordinated voluntary wages policy. In accepting the resolution, TUC General Secretary George Woodcock recalled that at the conference of executive committees earlier that year it had been agreed that the TUC should put emphasis upon attempts to improve the position of the low paid. 'This has always been our policy in general terms. We have given it a more precise content', he said.

In its 1968 Economic Review,[12] which was endorsed by a conference of union executive committees in February of that year, the TUC General Council began to spell out the tactical considerations flowing from this new policy. It saw three main avenues of approach. First, the TUC would seek to secure the broad agreement of the Confederation of British Industries for the establishment of a £15 minimum earnings guarantee for a 40 hour week for adult males and the commitment of the CBI to recommend this objective to its employers' associations. Second, negotiations between unions and employers in particular industries to examine improvements in organizations, labour utilization and wages structures with the specific aim of raising productivity and the earnings of lower paid workers. Third, the TUC would discuss with Government what it could do to promote this objective; the Government might act on a selective basis to promote development in low earnings areas and 'achievement of the objective might also involve enforcement action at a later stage at least in some industries.' The following month the TUC took the initiative on the first approach by raising the issue of the £15 minimum earnings guarantee with the CBI; the response was not encouraging. The CBI said that among the questions which would need to be considered were 'the social and economic justification for such a step and the basis for the figure selected as the objective' and the need to assess how many workers would be affected by the proposals. The only agreement reached was that the TUC and the CBI should jointly collect available information to make an examination of the characteristics of low paid workers.

The inability of the TUC General Council to provoke the employers, through the CBI, into action on a combined attack on low pay strengthened the tendency within the trade union Movement which—as evidenced by the statement in the 1968 Economic Review that enforcement action at a later stage might be required—stressed the need for positive Government action against low pay. At the 1968 annual Congress this tendency emerged in a resolution, moved by Alec Donnett of the General and Municipal Workers' Union, which called on the Government and the TUC to develop a comprehensive strategy against low pay and added: 'Congress calls upon the Government to investigate the possibility of buttressing the TUC's proposal for a national minimum by introducing legislation.'

Although the resolution was passed by the Congress the debate was in very low key and the possibility it posed of a legally enforceable minimum wage attracted no comment. The effects of the resolution, however, soon made themselves felt at much higher levels. Within three months of the Congress representatives of the General Council, in a meeting with the Secretary of State for Employment and Productivity and other Government Ministers, were arguing that despite the emphasis on incomes policy over the past four years there had been no significant improvement in the relative position of low paid workers. Legislative action, they said, might have to be taken to achieve a national minimum wage, with a timetable linked to the introduction of equal pay. The Minister admitted that the Government's policy had had little effect on low pay and—surprising for a Government which had introduced statutory control of wage increases—argued as a defence that the Government could not compel negotiators to give high priority to low paid workers and that the 'normal collective bargaining process' did not naturally work in the direction of eliminating low pay.

A few months later, in its 1969 Economic Review,[13] the General Council pressed home its arguments in a section which gave more detailed attention to low pay than had any of the previous reviews. After examining the available information, which it described as inadequate, it concluded there was 'no doubt about the widespread extent of low pay.' A useful by-product of the incomes policy was that it had at least directed more attention to the problem; but the real question was whether the operation of incomes policy had resulted in any significant improvement in the relative position of low paid workers, said the General Council. On the basis of movements of earnings between October 1964 and April 1968 the General Council concluded: 'Experience in the period in which incomes policy has been operating does not appear to have been significantly different from that in the preceding period . . . While, therefore, Congress has continued to assert the need for action to improve the relative position of low paid workers it is doubtful whether collective bargaining alone is likely to achieve this in the short run.' Having made this frontal assault on the inadequacies of the Government's incomes policy to assist the low paid, and half admitted the inability of the trade unions to resolve the problem speedily within the context of the traditional collective bargaining process, the General Council put forward its alternative.

'The foregoing analysis strengthens the General Council's view that a prior need is to promote the rationalization of industry with, as a concomitant, the effective development of collective bargaining to raise the living standards of the people whose well-being has been bounded by the inefficiency of the industries in which they work. It is also necessary to make improvements in the structure of the tax and social security systems, extending if necessary to the establishment of a national minimum wage backed by statutory action. These two approaches are complementary, although their impact on different industries will vary. Both fit naturally into a more progressive definition of incomes policy, geared to the collective bargaining methods and purposes of trade unions. They also offer the Government a more positive role in helping to secure greater industrial efficiency and rising living standards.'

The Government's response to growing trade union demands for positive measures to overcome low pay was to commission an inter-departmental working party of civil servants to examine the social, industrial and economic implications of introducing a national minimum wage. The working party's report[14] was published as a

Green Paper in May 1969 and was markedly unenthusiastic about the proposition. While largely confined to a description of the problems involved in the introduction of a national minimum wage the report questioned its effectiveness on the grounds that it would probably be a less efficient means of relieving poverty than would selective social benefits related to individual needs. The TUC reacted to this report in two ways. First, the General Council set up a working party of TUC staff and trade union research officers to survey the whole problem of low pay and the possibilities of establishing a national minimum wage as a solution to that problem. Second, at the annual Congress in September 1969, a resolution was carried which reaffirmed the principle of a £15 minimum wage for a 40 hour week established by the 1967 Congress and, during the debate, indicated that the minimum should now be £16·50 in order to maintain its real value in the light of price increases since 1967.

The TUC working party report[15] was published early in 1970 and, after examining the information on low pay in the light of the New Earnings Survey conducted by the Department of Employment in 1968, outlined three areas where action could be taken. The first was a number of ways the collective bargaining process could assist the low paid—such as productivity and efficiency arrangements, improved job content through regrading, training and promotion opportunities, examination of pay structures to establish fair relationships between groups of workers on the basis of overtime, bonus systems and incremental scales, and the use of minimum earnings guarantees. The second was the use of a national minimum wage, which the report suggested might take a statutory form, or a voluntary form agreed and implemented in consultation with the CBI, or the form of a specified trade union objective. The third area was the way in which tax and social security systems could be modified to assist the low paid. The report noted that the £16·50 figure adopted by the 1969 annual Congress could be justified in relation to social security benefits, through supplementary allowances and rent grants, paid to a man and wife with one child. It commented: 'This approach has the merit of relating the definition to an existing standard of need and would thereby ensure that a person in work does not receive less than someone drawing supplementary benefit.' The report also pointed out that alternative definitions of low pay were those based on a fixed proportion of national average earnings—two-thirds, for example—or on the lowest decile, and added that there was no reason in principle why any one of these methods should be preferred to another and it would probably be appropriate to take them all into account when arriving at a figure.

The report was circulated to all TUC affiliated unions with a request for their comments; on the basis of those comments and the report itself the TUC General Council agreed on a six point course of action:[16]

1. To adopt £16·50 as the target minimum basic rate as a guideline for union negotiators in wages council sectors and similar low paid industries and to consider the possibility and desirability of an appropriately higher minimum or series of minima as a guideline for industry generally.
2. To monitor developments in relation to this guideline and to review policy at least annually in the light of developments, taking into account movements in average earnings and the cost of living.
3. To discuss with the union sides of negotiating bodies in particularly low paid sectors ways in which they could raise the earnings of their lower paid members, including the extent to which these policies could be facilitated through the adoption of appropriate guidelines and targets.
4. To draw the attention of the Government to the guidelines which the General Council was recommending to unions, directing particular attention to those sectors where the Government had a prime responsibility—notably national and local government services, other public services such as the health service and Wages Councils.
5. To inform the CBI of the General Council's policy and to ask the CBI to recommend to its members this policy of improving the position of low paid workers in industry generally through the adoption of TUC targets.

6. To defer a decision on whether it would be useful for the Government to introduce further statutory backing for a national minimum wage and to review this position 'at an appropriate time in the light of experience.'

Coinciding with this process of development towards a definite policy on low pay by the TUC, relations between the Government and the TUC General Council in the area of incomes policy had reached rock bottom. When the General Council met Employment Secretary Mrs. Barbara Castle in December 1969 it refused to discuss in detail the draft of a White Paper (*Productivity*, *Prices and Incomes Policy after 1969*) because it did not wish the Government to think there was any prospect of the TUC endorsing the White Paper, either in whole or in part. This rebuff by the General Council came at a time when the Government, five years after launching its incomes policy, was making a very belated attempt to inject into it at least a paper recognition that there was a need to do something about low pay. The 1969 White Paper, for example, made the astonishing assertion that 'from the beginning' the Government incomes policy had tried to give the community an opportunity to improve the position of low paid workers. In a detailed section, the White Paper argued that one of the weaknesses of free collective bargaining had been its inability to solve the problem of low pay; a statement not without some historical justification but completely overlooking the fact that during the previous five years the Government's interference with free collective bargaining had not made any contribution to solving the problem. Rejecting the idea of a national minimum wage, the White Paper pinned its hopes on a strengthening of trade union organization amongst the lower paid and co-operation between unions and employers to help low paid workers achieve higher earnings by sharply raising their productivity. The Government, it said, would ask the NBPI to make special studies of low pay industries and it would invite unions and employers to join with the Government to work out solutions to the problems of those low paid workers who had been unjustifiably left behind in what it called the scramble of wage bargaining. The White Paper made clear, however, that this solution would have to be within the context of an incomes policy which embraced an imposed norm and included statutory powers over wages.

When the White Paper was published the General Council issued a statement which said that the proposals were unacceptable to trade unions because they were based on statutory interference which was at best irrelevant and at worst would hinder the development of a coherent policy for collective bargaining and incomes. The General Council pointed to the conspicuous contrast between the White Paper's detailed treatment of wages and the absence of any reference to high salaries, unearned incomes and the incomes of highly paid professional and self-employed persons. If at any time the Government developed a longer-term approach within a radically different framework from the hitherto restrictive incomes policy it could count on the co-operation of the unions, concluded the General Council. When, early in 1970, the Department of Employment and Productivity gave the General Council a list of seven industries where the NBPI might study low pay—as proposed in the White Paper—the General Council responded by asking the Government to declare what it thought constituted a satisfactory minimum wage for the workers in question, particularly as the Government itself had a direct responsibility for many of them.

The TUC's scepticism was confirmed when the reports on the three groups—hospital ancillary workers, laundry and dry cleaning and contract cleaners—eventually chosen for study were published by the NBPI in April 1971. The NBPI added a fourth report, *General Problems of Low Pay*,[17] explaining that on the basis of its in-depth studies of the three selected groups the General Report enabled it to discuss the theoretical and practical problems involved in identifying and attempting to raise low pay. Like the White Paper in which it originated, this NBPI report opened with the astonishing claim: 'The idea that the prices and incomes policy should be used to tackle the problem of low pay was present from its inauguration.' But, apart from a few selective quotations from a succession of White Papers, the report was unable to produce much evidence of the way in which the Government's policy had made any significant contribution to solving the problem of low pay. Indeed, in its conclusions to the report the NBPI was moved to confess: 'It is apparent from our studies that what little improvement took place in the relative position of the low-paid in the earlier years of the prices and incomes policy was later lost. This does not mean that another attempt to help the low paid in the context of a prices and incomes policy would inevitably fail. There are many factors which contributed to the lack of success of this aspect of the policy in 1965–70, including for example the intrinsic difficulty of the task, the shortage of experience in tackling it, the lack of consensus as to what constitutes low pay and the difficult economic circumstances in which the policy was operating.'

Considering this was written more than five years after the famous Joint Declaration of Intent, which marked the opening of incomes policy, and represented the first attempt of the NBPI to really get to grips with the fundamental problems of low pay, and bearing in mind the constant attempts of the trade unions to turn the Government's attention to low pay, it is small wonder that the report provoked a somewhat derisory response from many trade unionists and ultimately came to be viewed as a very sad epitaph to a Labour Government which had missed the opportunities presented to it.

4. The Politics Restated

> Some of these people who talk so touchingly of the low paid worker problem are the very people who want us to return to the economic and bargaining circumstances that produced them in the first place.
>
> TOM BRADLEY

In practical political terms the NBPI report on the *General Problems of Low Pay* was of no real significance. By the time it was published the Labour Government had been defeated and replaced by a Tory Government which had made opposition to a formalized and statutory incomes policy one of the features of its election programme. On taking office one of the first acts of the Tory Government had been to disband the Labour Government's incomes policy and to serve notice to quit on the NBPI, allowing it to remain in existence just long enough to produce its report on low pay.

In the field of collective bargaining, too, the reality of events had overtaken the theorizing of the NBPI. In September 1970 the three unions organizing local authority manual workers, who had been described as low paid by the NBPI nearly three-and-a-half years earlier, had decided to take matters into their own hands and had staged a six week strike in support of the TUC target of a £16·50 minimum wage and as a result had secured an increase of £2·50 to take them to within 25p of their objective. Speaking at the 1970 annual Congress a few days before the strike started, Alan Fisher, General Secretary of NUPE, described the conflict as of vital concern to every union in the country. The three unions, he said, were involved in the first frontal attack on low pay and for the first time they were pursuing an objective set out by the TUC General Council, which had said exactly what it expected unions to achieve in their efforts to wipe out low pay. The success of the local authority manual workers' strike was personally condemned by the Tory Prime Minister, Edward Heath, in a television broadcast. Like many others, he was painfully aware that the strike was a warning that low paid workers were developing a fighting capacity and that it had done more to focus public attention on the problem of low pay than five years of an incomes policy which lacked an essential ingredient.

For its part the TUC, following the election of the Tory Government in 1970, continued to develop its policy on low pay very much along the lines it had set out in the later years of the Labour Government. The General Council initiated a series of discussions with unions organizing in low pay sectors and directed particular attention to the limitations which Wages Councils imposed on efforts to improve low pay, At the 1971 annual Congress a resolution, proposed by Harry Urwin of the Transport and General Workers' Union, pledged the support of the TUC for unions seeking to establish a basic minimum wage of £20 a week and called for priority to be given to the need to raise the earnings of workers receiving less than the national average. In its 1972 Economic Review the General Council measured the £20 objective against the formula of supplementary benefit standards and two-thirds of average earnings and concluded in each case that the figure could be justified. It subsequently urged the Tory Government, in much the same way as it had urged the Labour Government, to accept the need for a unified policy on low pay; with a target of not less than two-thirds average earnings for all workers together with programmes for income and job security, the establishment of a National Manpower Board, the need for local arbitration on terms and conditions of employment in designated areas and for special action in Wages Council industries. At the same time the General Council recommended unions to consider ways in which they could achieve a more co-ordinated approach to low pay problems, embracing economic, structural and collective bargaining decisions.

Statistically the General Council could point to some areas of very limited success in improving the position of some low paid workers through the collective bargaining process, but what was still lacking was the massive breakthrough over a broad front which many unions had been seeking for some years. Evidence of niggling impatience was apparent in a resolution, proposed by Alf Allen, General Secretary of the Union of Shop, Distributive and Allied Workers, at the 1972 annual Congress which called upon the General Council to 'press more vigorously for the establishment of a national minimum wage.' Although it was not specifically articulated during the debate, this call was undoubtedly an echo of the theme which had constantly emerged in trade union discussions on low pay: that in addition to efforts it made through collective bargaining in specific industries, the trade union Movement should be working on a much wider canvas, and using different methods, to establish a minimum wage which had national application as the central feature of a campaign to eliminate low pay.

The new Tory Government continued to direct attention towards the low paid through the social security system, extending the policies of the previous Labour Government which believed that assistance to the low paid worker should be on an individual basis designed to meet family needs. The Tory solution was to introduce the Family Incomes Supplement, paid on a means-test basis to families with children where the income from employment fell below a level determined by the Government. As we will show in a later chapter, trade union objections to the Government's FIS proposals were many; it is sufficient to note at this point that the TUC General Council, in its 1971 Economic Review, said while it welcomed Government action to assist families in poverty it had the strongest reservations about FIS as a solution to the problem of inadequate incomes among wage earners. 'The family income supplement will comprise a direct and explicit subsidy to low wages, and may have the effect in lower paid industries of actually slowing down the progress of improvements in wage levels.' Trade union negotiators, nearer to the real firing line than the TUC, soon became painfully aware that FIS—and other means-tested assistance to the low paid—actually swallowed up pay increases which had been hard won through the collective bargaining process.

This point of difference between the trade unions and the Government rapidly became submerged, however, when the Tories, forgetting their pre-election objections to statutory incomes policy, introduced a 90 day wage freeze in November 1972 and followed this up with Stage 2 policy which imposed a statutory limit of £1 plus 4 per cent on pay increases. Seeking to justify this approach the Government claimed in a White Paper that its formula was 'designed to favour low paid workers for whom it would give a better deal than a single percentage limit.' The overall trade union reaction to this policy was, inevitably, hostile and is well enough documented not to need repeating. In relation to low pay, however, the General Council in a report[2] to a Special Trades Union Congress in March 1973, challenged the Government's contention that its Stage 2 formula would help the low paid. It pointed out that the formula 'could mean less than £2 a week for a worker earning £20, but £5 a week for someone earning nearly £5,000 a year.' The Government's policy, it argued, would perpetuate the existence of low paid industries, and it said that £25 was the minimum that a worker should receive in earnings for a normal week and the TUC 'would give priority to raising the standards of workers whose basic rates for the negotiated week of 40 hours or less (excluding overtime) are below £22·50.'

When the Government, in October 1973, published the details of the next step in its incomes policy, Stage 3, the response of the TUC General Council was equally cold. 'On low pay the Government's emphasis is still far too much on one group of workers making sacrifices in favour of another group,' it said. Spurning Government suggestions that it should join a new body to be set up to study low pay, the General Council said: 'Any special low pay body associated with the dead hand of the Pay Board would not have the confidence of the trade union Movement.' In a later, and more detailed, statement the General Council reaffirmed its refusal to join the new body and set out four ways in which the Government could make a direct contribution to tackling the problem of low pay. First, a considerable contribution could be made towards easing the problem of low pay if the Government would accept the target of a £25 minimum basic rate for a normal week, show willingness to apply this in areas directly under its control (the public sector) or under its influence (Wages Councils) and encourage negotiators to adopt this figure in other sectors. Second, the Government should take direct action to encourage economic development and structural change—for providing the framework within which problems of low pay could be tackled by those concerned. Third, the Government should remove obstacles to the effective operation of arbitration machinery. Particular attention should be given to the TUC proposal for local arbitration services to ensure that employers in low paid industries complied with the recognized terms and conditions of employment established by collective bargaining machinery for the trade or industry. Fourth, the Government should seriously examine TUC proposals for amendments to Wages Council legislation to facilitate abolition where this was considered necessary and to enable them to play a more positive role in eliminating the problem of low pay. In particular, there was need to replace existing restrictions on their operations with new terms of reference which would enable them to examine questions of efficiency, manpower, security and job and pay restructuring relevant to the problem of improving wages in line with the £25 target; and require them regularly to review progress towards the objective of developing voluntary collective bargaining throughout the sector, and to publish an annual report of progress in attaining these objectives. Needless to say, these proposals met with no response from the Government.

It was, perhaps, ironic that the Pay Board, which had been set up to administer the Tory Government's incomes policy, should have been chosen to write the epitaph on the Tory Government's low pay policy in the same way that the NBPI had performed a similar function for the Labour Government.

In March 1973 the conflict between the unions and the Government over Stage 2 incomes policy had reached a sharp point; the TUC General Council called a Special Congress to discuss strategy while hospital ancillary workers and civil servants were making history by taking industrial action aimed directly at the Government. In order to allay growing public concern that its policy was penalizing the low paid, the Government chose this time to ask the

Pay Board to examine the problem of pay relativities. In making its reference to the Board, the Government said: 'Within any system for the determination of pay, groups from time to time feel that they deserve special treatment in order, for example, to improve their relative position within the community or in relation to other parts of the same industry. If a policy for controlling inflation is to be effective and fair, it must have procedures for considering such claims objectively.'

Government spokesmen and their supporters used this reference to the Pay Board to justify their claims that their incomes policy was designed to give special consideration to the low paid. Many unions, though highly sceptical, decided to put these claims to the test and made detailed submissions to the Pay Board on behalf of specific groups of low paid workers. The unions representing hospital ancillary workers, for example, took their cue from the words used by the Government and told the Board that ancillary workers 'merit this special treatment in order to improve their relative position within the community.' In detailed evidence, both written and oral, they argued that the hospital workers were low paid in relation to national average earnings; were low paid in relation to the minimum income required to maintain a reasonable standard of life; and were low paid in relation to the social utility of the services they provided to the community.

When the Board's long-awaited report[3] eventually appeared, in January 1974, it proved to be very much a damp squib. In its only reference to the problem of low pay it commented that it was 'partly one of relativities and partly one of poverty.' It added: 'We doubt whether it would be possible for the problem of low pay to be handled entirely apart from that of relativities; but, as the Government have proposed that a separate tripartite body should be set up to deal with low pay, we do not think it would be appropriate for us to make recommendations on this subject at this stage.' Thus, not only did the Board skate over the issue which Tory politicians had claimed was central to their policy, it also overlooked the fact that months before the TUC General Council had told the Government that it would not participate in the new tripartite low pay body within the terms of reference set out by the Government.

However, in an historical re-enactment of the situation several years earlier, the Pay Board's report had little real significance in terms of practical politics. Within weeks of its publication the Tory Government chose to hold a general election using 'extremist' trade unions as their main argument for the return of a strengthened Tory Government which would then pursue 'firm but fair' policies against the unions—an argument which was rejected by the electorate.

The defeat of the Tories in the 1974 General Election brought to an end a decade in which low paid workers had seen much discussion of their problems but little progress in resolving them. It was a decade in which a Labour Government foundered on the rocks of an incomes policy which gave little consideration to the need to develop a policy to eliminate low pay, in which the trade union Movement had become increasingly aware of the problems of low paid workers and made serious but limited attempts to meet them, and in which a Tory Government had once again demonstrated the impossibility of combating low pay within a social and economic framework founded on inequality. Like all historical surveys, the lessons of that decade point a way for the future; and the direction in which those lessons point was indicated in two debates towards the end of 1973, one at the annual Trades Union Congress and the other at the Labour Party Annual Conference. Both debates were initiated by NUPE in a serious attempt to raise the level of discussion on low pay, to give it a new sense of purpose and to set its sights on new objectives.

At the annual Congress the NUPE resolution, moved by its Research Officer Bernard Dix, expressed opposition to Government policies which allowed rising living costs to retard the growth of real wages, particularly those of lower paid workers, declared the determination of the TUC to establish a basic minimum wage of £25 for a standard working week and pledged support for any union seeking to secure this objective. In moving the resolution, which was passed without dissent, Bernard Dix said that there were two basic approaches to overcoming low pay: the trade union Movement could use its energies to establish a legal minimum wage of £25 a week or it could use its collective bargaining strength to win £25 a week in negotiations with employers.

'A legal minimum wage of £25 is only possible within the context of an overall economic policy which is designed to shift income and wealth to those areas where low pay is endemic. It requires a taxation policy which takes money away from those who've got it and gives it to those who haven't. It requires a policy of public ownership which, for example, uses the profits of a very lucrative drug industry to pay decent wages to hospital workers.' Such a policy, said Bernard Dix, was inconceivable within the context of Tory philosophy and would need to wait the election of a Labour Government committed to a Socialist programme. For this reason the tactics for the trade union Movement, in the circumstances where a Tory Government was in power, must be to use its bargaining strength to win a £25 minimum. It was for this reason the resolution emphasized the need for the TUC to give full support to unions struggling to win a £25 minimum wage through the collective bargaining process who got involved in strike action.

By presenting the argument in this fashion, NUPE was accepting the limitations placed on the trade union Movement at that time by a Tory Government but was deliberately raising the need for trade unions to pursue different tactics when a Labour Government was in power: it was posing the ultimate need for a political solution. The resolution at the Labour Party Conference,[4] moved by Alan Fisher, General Secretary of NUPE, pursued this tactic by turning the emphasis of the argument the other way round and spelling out to a Labour Party audience the need for the next Labour Government to give priority to the lower paid worker by producing a programme for the introduction of a legally enforceable minimum wage set at 80 per cent of average industrial earnings and reviewed annually (the percentage figure, incidentally and unfortunately, was included as part of a composite resolution and did not originate with NUPE).

In moving the resolution, Alan Fisher said that it sought a political solution to a problem which required urgent attention by the next Labour Government. It was a political issue for three reasons. First, many low paid workers were employed by the Government; the next Labour Government must acknowledge this and assume direct responsibility for increasing their pay.

Second, it was 'nonsense' to think that a strategy for ending low pay could be effective without political action; the redistribution of wealth, reform of taxation, the curbing of increases in food prices, rents and transport costs all required political action. Third, low pay could not be ended through collective bargaining alone; the bargaining power of workers in many low paid industries was not as great as that of workers in production industries.

'We have looked at the Labour Party's programme and we have asked ourselves: "Is the Party committed to a coherent strategy for ending low pay through such political action?" And the answer is "no", the commitment to give justice to low paid workers in the programme is in the context of operating a voluntary incomes policy. This is not ending injustice. It is just a formula to ensure that low paid workers do not fall further behind during the operating of that incomes policy.

'If this Party is serious about redistributing wealth then it must grasp the nettle of low pay. Without a statutory framework for making progress towards a minimum wage, this redistributive policy will fail.'

Turning to the Labour Party's proposals for a standing Royal Commission on incomes distribution, Alan Fisher said that it would take many years for the results of such an enquiry to make any impression on earnings. 'Enough is known about the general problems of low pay for the next Labour Government to act quickly and decisively . . . What we are concerned about is tackling the problem of all lower paid workers, not by platitudes—we have had plenty of those in the past—but by a positive commitment to legislation on a statutory minimum wage.

'I do not believe that the return to free collective bargaining in this country will in itself solve the problem of the unfair distribution of incomes. There needs to be action by the Government to ensure that a safety net is established at a standard below which no one shall be allowed to fall and that is what this resolution seeks to achieve.'

The resolution was opposed from the floor of the conference by John Boyd, of the Amalgamated Union of Engineering Workers, who confessed that it was 'a very embarrassing experience' for him to speak against the resolution at the request of his Union's delegation.

Putting forward the main reason for the AUEW's opposition, John Boyd said: 'To support this resolution many unions in the TUC, including my own, would really require to commit a somersault because one of the main bastions of our opposition to the present Government has been their interference with collective bargaining and our right as democrats representing workers to be free to freely negotiate within collective bargaining arrangements. So it seems ludicrous if on the one hand we are going to conduct such a strong militant campaign as we have this past three or four years and then say "yes" to the next Labour Government, "We want you to interfere with collective bargaining and we want you to lay down a legal minimum".'

Speaking on behalf of the Party National Executive and urging the conference to reject the resolution Tom Bradley, an MP sponsored by the Transport Salaried Staffs Association, made a similar point: 'There are some difficulties in very rightly opposing government intervention in wages on the one hand and appealing for their assistance on the other.' He emphasized the role of social security and said: 'It may well be that at the end of the day social policy offers a better prospect for the relief of the poor because of the variations in the circumstances of individuals. The chronically sick, the incapacitated, the unemployed, the retired, the handicapped, are all part and parcel of this gigantic problem of poverty that exists in certain sections of our society.'

When the votes were taken at the end of the debate the big battalions dutifully fell into line and the resolution was defeated by a three to one majority. Even at this stage, the Party leadership had apparently learned nothing from the failures of the Labour Government's policies between 1964 and 1970. Equally, many trade unionists had not reached the level of political understanding where they could differentiate between a negative policy of unilateral Government wage restraint which would maintain existing economic and social relationships and a policy jointly generated by the unions and a Socialist Government intended to favour the working class by assisting the low paid. However, the fact that the resolution attracted nearly 1½ million votes, despite the opposition of the Party leadership and some of the bigger trade unions, demonstrated that the construction of a national minimum wage as a solution to the problem of low pay had become a political issue with a substantial degree of support which could serve as the base from which to make further advances.

5. Means and Ends

> A man's pay does much more than provide him with his shelter. It says something about his skill and his responsibility, his status and his achievement, his relationships with his neighbours and the rest of the community. In a way it fixes his place in society.
>
> SIR FRANK FIGGURES

Over the past decade, during which low pay has become a topic for constant discussion if not commensurate action, what attempts have been made to tackle the problem at Government level have centred on the provision of means-tested benefits as a supplement to the wage income of low paid families rather than on direct action to raise the wage levels themselves. As a result there is now a multitude of these means-tested benefits available to families where the bread winner is in full-time work but whose pay falls below specific levels; the main benefits are the Family Income Supplement (FIS), rent and rate rebates, free school meals, school uniform grants, education maintenance allowances, free welfare foods (milk and vitamins for nursing and expectant mothers), free medical prescriptions and free dental and optical treatment.

Employers have not been slow to use the existence of these benefits to resist wage claims designed to improve the position of the low paid worker. In 1971, when FIS was first introduced, both the local authority employers and the management side of the Ancillary Staffs Council made direct reference to FIS and other benefits when responding to union claims for pay increases for local authority manual workers and hospital ancillary workers.

The local authority employers drew attention to the conclusion of the NBPI that tax and social security measures were an effective means of redistributing income to favour the low paid, and commented that this '. . . emphasizes the point that we must take into account changes in social security arrangements in evaluating any change in relative positions. Here the most important change is the Family Incomes Supplement which was introduced in 1971 specifically to deal with the problem of low earnings from employment.' The management side of the Ancillary Staffs Council actually criticised the unions for failing to include any reference to FIS in their claim. It continued: 'It is for the Government of the day, in pursuit of its social and fiscal policies, to decide the balance between workers and state beneficiaries, those with and without family responsibilities, rich and poor, etc. We shall only confuse negotiations which are already complex enough, if we become involved in such issues. Our task in negotiation is to ensure that the National Health Service pays a fair rate for the job.' It was not a coincidence that the local authority employers made exactly the same point when they said, '. . . poverty is best tackled by specific measures which take into account differences in earnings and differences in family circumstances . . . It is not therefore for individual negotiating bodies, but is rather a matter for Government in pursuit of social and fiscal policies.'

It was not without significance that both of these employers were in the public sector and directly exposed to Government influence when dealing with pay claims. Their equal insistence that social and fiscal policies were the principal method of dealing with low pay was evidence that the Government's policy was successfully being transmitted to the negotiating table. Therefore, as many trade unionists had predicted, the increasing reliance by Government on means-tested benefits to overcome low pay was distorting the bargaining process by allowing employers to import these considerations when dealing with claims aimed at improving the position of the low paid. The ability of unions to make significant improvements in the wages of low paid workers was therefore limited through an imposed coalition of Government and employer attitudes.

Apart from their effect on the collective bargaining process much of the general discussion surrounding the use of means-tested benefits for low paid families has concentrated on their effectiveness. The benefits are administered by a variety of public agencies; many become operative at different levels of income; the onus is on the low paid to claim them and demonstrate their eligibility to the satisfaction of the various officials administering them; there is insufficient public knowledge of some of the benefits; claiming them involves a complex process of form filling; many potential beneficiaries have an objection to what they construe as 'charity'—all of these reasons, and many others, have been advanced by critics of the system to argue that it is ineffective because it has a low level of take-up. In other words, with not one of the benefits is there more than an 80 per cent take-up by those who have an entitlement and with many of them the take-up rate is very much below this figure.

There is a further frequent criticism of the spread of means-tested benefits insofar as they affect the low paid. This is the poverty trap created by the coincidence of means-tested benefits and the level at which income tax becomes payable and which means, for low paid workers at certain earnings levels, that a fairly modest increase in pay can lift them above the scope of the benefits while taking them over the tax threshold; thus leaving them little better off—in some cases worse off—than they were before they received the pay increase. Michael Meacher, the Labour MP for Oldham, has made an exhaustive study of this problem and in his evidence to the Wilberforce Inquiry, at the time of the 1972 miners' strike, he presented a formidable indictment of the factors which have created the poverty trap. He showed, for example, that a married man, with two children, who had weekly earnings of £19 and who received a pay increase of £1 would be 10p a week worse off because of the poverty trap factors. He summarized his conclusions as follows:[1]

'There is clear evidence that the combined interaction of three factors is producing a poverty trap for the lower-paid from which they cannot escape without disproportionately large wage-increases. These factors are:

1. The sharp drop in the tax threshold leading to an enormously disproportionate increase in the tax-take relative to gross wages, especially for the lower-paid in recent years.
2. The considerable extension of the coverage of means-tested benefits which, if rejected, loses the only non-market assistance available to supplement low wages, and which, if accepted, very markedly diminishes the capacity to make any further real gains in the market.
3. The acceleration of price inflation leading to a large upward float of money wages without more than a marginal increase in purchasing power.

'It is the conjunction of these factors rather than any one in isolation which constitutes the poverty trap and which, even if not fully understood, is increasingly leading to an accurate awareness that only very substantial increases in low wages, that take workers beyond the area where these factors concur, offer a way out.'

It is interesting to note that, when it suits their convenience, employers will argue that considerations of the poverty trap should be discounted in pay negotiations while at the same time they will insist that social and fiscal benefits intended to assist low paid families should be taken into account. We have previously mentioned how the management side of the Ancillary Staffs Council, in their response to the 1971 pay claim, made a strong point of the availability of FIS and similar benefits. They also argued, however: '. . . as employers, we do not accept that changes in the level of social security benefits, rebate schemes, tax changes, etcetera should be taken into account in wage settlements.' Doubtless they would claim that this is a logical extension of their attitude that these are matters for Government in pursuit of its social and fiscal policies, but to trade unionists it looks suspiciously like another example of employers wanting to have their cake and eat it.

So far we have seen three criticisms of the Government policy of restorting to means-tested benefits as the main method of supplementing the incomes of low paid families. First, it distorts the collective bargaining process and handicaps the unions in their efforts to raise low wages. Second, it is ineffective because it fails to reach many of the people it is supposed to reach. Third, it combines with the tax structure and price inflation to worsen the relative position of many low paid families. These are legitimate criticisms which by themselves present a very strong case against the policies that have been pursued over the past ten years. They are, however, general criticisms which can be—and have been—made by many people who stand at very different points in the political spectrum. We have a further criticism which, from our committed viewpoint, we consider to be much more fundamental.

To many Socialists it is a matter for considerable concern that the major responsibility for the present emphasis on means-tested income supplements as the principal method of providing assistance to the low paid worker rests with the Labour Party. Throughout its term of office as Government in the period 1964–70 the Labour Party failed, as we have shown in a previous chapter, to respond to growing trade union pressure to develop its incomes policy as a weapon to combat low pay. Instead the Government pinned its faith on the ability of social and fiscal policies to cope with the problem of low pay within the wider context of family poverty and in doing so it committed a serious political error.

The evidence to support our argument is readily available and a few examples will be sufficient to demonstrate its validity. The 1966 White Paper[2] is an early reference point to developing Labour Government attitudes with its clear statement: 'As in practice the needs of individual workers are largely determined by the extent of their family commitments, the Government will continue to give a high priority to measures specifically designed to meet family needs.' The agencies of Government responsible for administering this policy provided support with comments which have seen considerable quotation. A report[3] by the Department of Employment and Productivity in 1969 concluded: 'The system of taxes and benefits operates in a way that benefits persons with low pay who have family commitments. The lower the pay the greater the benefit. Thus the system of taxation and social security benefits takes account of personal circumstances in a way which a national minimum could not do.' The NBPI, with its dying breath, echoed this view when in its report[4] *General Problems of Low Pay* it said '. . . while past experience indicates the difficulty of raising the gross earnings of low paid workers in relation to those of other workers, the tax and social security system has provided an effective means of redistributing net income in a way which favours the low paid.'

For their part, Labour Ministers were extremely sensitive to criticisms that the Government's incomes policy was not making any impression on the problem of low pay and continually emphasized that low pay was primarily a 'welfare' problem. An explicit statement of the Government's attitude was given by Harold Walker, Under Secretary of State for Employment and Productivity, when he told the House of Commons in March 1969: 'It is not a primary function of the Government's prices and incomes policy to redistribute incomes. Social and fiscal policies have their role to play in this and they are doing it.'[5] David Ennals, Minister of State at the Department of Health and Social Security, was even more vigorous in his defence of the Government when speaking at a meeting of the Child Poverty Action Group a year later: 'To say that the poor are getting poorer is a cynical comment which stands the truth on its head. The poor are not getting poorer and I have the figures to prove it. The incomes of low earnings families with several children have increased much more than average earnings. The Government have doubled family allowances. They have introduced the rate rebate scheme. Twice the number of children now get free school meals than in 1964. The family man on a low wage is now better off—both absolutely and relatively.'[6]

This kind of advocacy by Labour Ministers of selective and means-tested methods as the primary way of assisting the low paid worker was much more than the spontaneous reactions of public speakers under pressure in a sensitive area; it characterized an important shift in the Labour Party's overall political approach.

From the general election of 1945 until the mid-1960s the central theme of the Labour Party had been the need to construct and pursue a policy which would establish and extend what was popularly known as the Welfare State. The basis of that Welfare State was equality of social rights and the elimination of means-tests as a qualification for those rights: the objective was the establishment of social equality as much as the elimination of economic inequality. By placing increasing reliance on means-tested benefits as the principal method of assisting the families of low paid workers the Labour Government of 1964–70 reversed that policy in a way which, although it attracted very little attention at the time, was of considerable significance.

Defenders of the Labour Government will argue that, given the external economic circumstances during the period in which it was in office, there was no alternative open to it: that the need to give priority to policies designed to secure a healthy balance of payments dictated a revision of many traditional Labour Party policies and that the extension of selectivity and means-testing in social policies was one of the compromises the Government was forced to make in order to exist. We would challenge that view, and argue that by subordinating its social objectives to what it saw as immediate economic strategy in response to pressures from financial and business institutions at home and abroad the Labour Government capitulated to economic orthodoxy; missed the opportunity to relate its social policies to economic needs and to use them as a spearhead to attack the real problems confronting the country; and in the process weakened its traditional power amongst the advanced workers in the trade unions. Equally important, it opened the way for its Tory successor to extend the principles of selectivity and means-testing and helped to create the climate in which people like the renegade Labour Party member Dr. Rhodes Boyson, now Tory MP for Brent North, could seriously suggest a 'free enterprise' system of welfare services which would be organized to provide 'money or vouchers to enable the truly handicapped or deprived to buy their goods and services in the market place where competition keeps down prices, restricts bureaucracy and makes suppliers responsive to consumer preferences.'[7]

At this point we must make it quite clear that we fully recognize that fiscal and social policies have a part—an important part—to play in the campaign to eliminate low pay and to redistribute incomes in the process. On this we are in accord with the TUC when it said: 'Improvements in the structure of tax and social benefits should be seen as complementary with, rather than as an alternative to, methods of raising minimum earnings levels. This is because taxation and social policies provide a means of relating income to differing needs in a way which improved earnings cannot; they can for example allow for differences in family size, reduced earning power due to disablement or interruptions in employment.' These improvements can be of a relatively simple nature: such as a minimum earned income allowance which would enable income tax reductions to be concentrated at the lower end of the scale and increased family allowances, extended to the first child in the family, combined with a claw back system wich removes the increased benefits from the higher paid. Such improvements, which have long been advocated by the TUC, would be of real assistance to low paid families and their adoption—combined with an elimination of means-tested benefits—would mark a return to the original methods of the Labour Party in pursuit of its social objectives.

We are convinced that it is essential for the Labour Party to take decisions in this direction in the area of social and fiscal policies as a deliberate repudiation of its past aberrations and as a conscious political act in the development of a Socialist programme to eliminate low pay which has a national minimum wage as its focal point.

In recent years, in part arising out of its policy and in part feeding on the extension of that policy, there has been an increasing tendency within the Labour Party—and within the trade unions for that matter—to emphasize the economic problems of low pay and to concentrate energies on diverting a small segment of the national income to help alleviate those problems through the social security system. But low pay is not merely an economic problem, it is also a social condition which has profound implications, not only for the low paid themselves but for the kind of society in which we all live. Low pay does not mean just a shortage of cash, it marks out social status. All of the statistical evidence available shows that most children of low paid families are on a conveyor belt which leads from secondary modern school to unskilled job and that they have virtually no change of further education; that they are more likely to live in overcrowded houses which lack modern amenities; that their fathers are more likely to be absent from work due to illness or injury and in old age they are more likely to be chronically sick and to die at an earlier age. These factors are more than personal problems for the low paid families, they help to determine relationships within society. And just as the existence of low pay helps to determine social divisions so, too, will the methods chosen to eliminate it. The reliance on means-tested benefits as the main method of alleviating low pay may bring some marginal financial relief, but at the same time it not only stigmatises and further diminishes the social status of the low paid but also helps to perpetuate the kind of divisions within the working class which should have no place in the vocabulary of Socialists. We believe that the real alternative for the Labour Party and the trade unions is to use a national minimum wage as the major offensive weapon against low pay and to complement this with social and fiscal policies, which are universal in application, to take care of individual circumstances. This method will not only eliminate the economic problem of low pay, it will also help smash down the social barriers associated with it.

6. A Case for Control

Industries should be left to settle their wages in the market.

JO GRIMOND

At the beginning of this book we said that low pay continued to exist in Britain because those who were, or who had been, in a position to do something about it had failed to act because they were constipated by economic and political orthodoxy. Nowhere is the truth of this statement more apparent than in the arguments used by those who oppose the introduction of a national minimum wage on the grounds that, however desirable its objectives may be and however honourable the motives of those who advocate it, the practical consequences of its economic disadvantages would outweigh any social advantages it might have.

Whatever the form of words used, these arguments rest on the proposition that by far the most important factor which determines, and will continue to determine, the levels of wages is the interaction of market forces. Put very crudely, this starts from the point that whether wages are high or low depends on supply and demand in the labour market. There are, however, a number of qualifications. The demand for labour is a derived demand: employers do not want labour for its own sake but for the power it has to produce goods and services. The demand for labour, therefore, depends on the demand for the goods and services which the employer provides. The demand for these goods and services depends in turn on a number of other factors, and not least the price level at which the employer is able to sell the product in quantities sufficient to bring him an acceptable profit—which is what the whole complex process of production is all about so far as he is concerned. If, say our opponents, an employer is placed under a legal obligation to pay a minimum wage the advantage that wage brings to the individual worker must be set against the repercussions this will have on this whole range of connected matters: this is the interaction of market forces. In short, our opponents are saying that the real test of the value of introducing a national minimum wage must be determined not by the benefits it gives to low paid workers but by how employers react and the effects their reactions have on the economy as a whole as it in turn responds to the needs of the employers.

Using this general theoretical foundation, which is based on the acceptance of orthodox capitalist economics, as their take-off point our opponents project a devastating sequence of likely events which is intended to demolish the case for a national minimum wage by showing that it would either create unemployment, increase prices, reduce profits or produce a combination of all three at the same time.

This catalogue of catastrophes, they say, would unfold as employers reacted to the increased labour costs which would follow the introduction of a national minimum wage. Some employers would immediately respond in a traditional fashion by reducing the size of their labour forces; the resulting unemployment would hit hardest at those industries which contain the largest concentrations of low paid workers and at those areas of the country where unemployment levels are already above the national average and where earnings tend to be lower as a consequence. The overall result would be a general rise in unemployment which would tend to depress the average level of earnings.

Putting up prices to meet the cost of higher pay would not necessarily solve the problem of unemployment, because higher prices would cause the demand for some products to drop and the employers would then cut back their labour forces to meet this situation. In any event, the increased prices—coming at a time when Britain is already faced with a breath-taking rate of inflaton—would feed into the economy and help wipe out any gains made by the lower paid and worsen their relative position as higher paid workers secured pay increases to meet rising prices. If an employer did not reduce his labour force or put up prices his profit levels would be squeezed, and in many cases this would eventually drive him out of business, thereby creating more unemployment. It would be open to employers to cover the cost of paying the national minimum wage by introducing labour saving machinery and taking other steps to raise productivity, but these measures would take time, would require additional finance at a time when profits were being hard pressed and in any case might eventually result in a situation where there were fewer job opportunities and higher unemployment.

In addition to all of these problems, there is the fact that many low paid workers are to be found in the public services where there are no profits to be squeezed and where the nature of the work often places a limit on the possibility of making any significant improvements in productivity. If the level of these services and their labour forces were maintained the cost of paying the national minimum wage would have to be passed on to the consumer in higher rates and taxes, which would add further twists to the inflationary spiral with all of its negative consequences for the low paid.

Such is the grim spectre presented by those who argue that, however well intentioned, a national minimum wage would provoke such a chain reaction of events that the total outcome would be of sufficient weight to tip the balance and send Britain's already unstable economy sliding headlong to disaster. Ignoring for the moment the natural pessimism and over-exaggeration which seems to characterize orthodox economists, let us be perfectly honest and admit that all of these consequences could well follow the introduction of a national minimum wage. We can go even further, and say that they undoubtedly would occur if nothing positive was done to offset them. This admission, however, strengthens our case rather than weakens it; because it is nothing more than a restatement of our belief that an uncontrolled market economy—

the ideal capitalism of the classical economists—is absolutely incapable of solving the problem of low pay. It is because we are prepared to make such an admission that we insisted, right at the beginning of this book, that low pay is a political question and that its solution can be found and presented only within a political context.

Looked at from this standpoint it is inconceivable that the Tory Party, with its firm commitment to what it chooses to call a free enterprise philosophy, could ever accommodate the necessary fundamental changes in economic policy if the problem of low pay is to be solved. It is equally impossible for the Liberal Party, despite its more recent advocacy of a national minimum earnings level among the shower of disjointed proposals it has thrown up in absence of a coherent policy, to embrace the radical economic attitudes needed as the base from which to attack low pay. The political answer, if it is to be presented at all, must come from the Labour Party which—despite its failings in the 1964–70 period—alone has the immediate potential to construct an economic policy designed to frustrate the adverse interaction of market forces and thus present a framework within which a national minimum wage can operate effectively as the primary method of eliminating low pay. The Labour Party can do this because it is a Party which has an unashamed interventionist tradition: it owes its existence to the fact that it rejects the belief that economic and social affairs can be left to the free play of market forces. It is on the basis of that tradition that it can, and must, develop an attack on low pay.

Just as in the past the TUC has insisted that any incomes policy must fit within the context of an overall economic and social plan designed to realize the objectives of the trade union Movement so, too, must a policy for eliminating low pay. Because a national minimum wage raises the wider issues of employment, prices, profits and productivity its application must be considered in the setting of policies designed to tackle these matters; not only because they are relevant to low pay but because they are matters which are at the very centre of the total economic problem currently confronting Britain. The need for such an approach was apparent in the TUC's attitude when it told the Tory Government, at the end of 1973, that to assist in overcoming low pay the Government needed to take direct action to promote economic development and structural change and thus provide the environment within which the problems of low pay could be tackled. The prime need is for the TUC and the Labour Party, whether it is in Government or not, to reach a mutual agreement which sets out the details of such a policy arising from a commitment to the national minimum wage.

The starting points are already established in much of the existing policy and machinery; the first step must be to relate these fragmented policies to the specific objective of eliminating low pay and to compound them into a coherent and embracing policy.

In the inflationary situation that exists in Britain at the moment public attention is understandably directed towards prices. If a programme designed to introduce a national minimum wage is to win public support it must therefore be able to demonstrate that it will not add to inflationary pressures by raising prices. Is this a practical proposition, particularly when it is remembered that for several years governments have been unable to cope with the general problem of inflation, let alone handle an extra dimension introduced by a national minimum wage? The answer is to be found not in the incapacity of governments, but in their willingness to adopt policies designed to cope with inflation by acting directly against market forces. The TUC General Council pointed the way out when, in its talks on inflation with the Tory Government in July 1973, it stated without reservation: 'All prices must be legally and rigidly controlled,' and added that to achieve this objective the Government should immediately arm itself with the additional powers it needed to introduce such controls. As part of the strategy for countering any effects of the introduction of a national minimum wage on prices the need for such positive action by Government becomes more crucial. The rudiments of the machinery on which to build this control exist in the Price Commission, set up by the Tory Government under its Counter Inflation Act, which gives it the powers to 'restrict any prices or charges for the sale of goods or the performance of services in the course of business.' The Price Commission could be retained, or restored if it has been abolished, and its specific frame of reference—which is derived from the provisions of the codes drawn up from time to time by Parliament—strengthened and directed particularly to dealing with price increases arising out of the introduction of the national minimum wage. The extent to which an employer could increase prices, if at all, to meet higher wage costs would therefore be rigidly controlled by Government, which could decide on the precise level of control in the light of both the individual circumstances of particular employers and the overall economic situation. At the same time an effective system of local surveillance, based on a strengthened Weights and Measures Inspectorate equipped with immediate powers to control shop and service establishment prices and backed by a legal enforcement system in the Magistrates' Courts, would tighten up some of the loopholes which existed in the Tory Government's system. Measures such as these, coupled with the general attack on price inflation to which the Labour Party is already committed, would command wide public support and help to establish a sympathetic climate for the overall campaign against low pay. They would also bring tangible benefits to the low paid as part of the general process of halting price inflation.

With price controls limiting their ability to pass on to the consumer the cost of introducing the national minimum wage, employers would be faced with immediate pressure on their profit margins. In some cases this would have a valuable redistributive effect by slicing the fat off the back of high profit-low wage industries. Other firms, with narrower margins, would be forced to begin to consider either improving their efficiency or reducing their labour forces; one of the objects of the overall policy against low pay should be to encourage the former and discourage the latter. Again the rudiments of policy and machinery already exist which, if strengthened and given a new sense of purpose, could not only cope with the additional problems arising out of the introduction of the national minimum wage but could also make a general contribution to planned economic growth.

The National Economic Development Council and its associated Economic Development Committees, with their representation from unions, employers and Government, provide a natural arena for tackling the problems of manpower planning and productivity improvement in industries where low pay is a major factor and where the introduction of a national minimum wage would pose the need for quick action. The establishment of more EDCs directly related to low pay industries and an extension of their powers to give them a greater impact at the level of the individual enterprise would be a positive step in the overall programme to eliminate low pay. At the level of the NEDC itself the Government could make a new remit giving specific responsibility and powers to the NEDC to monitor continually the economic repercussions of the national minimum wage with particular reference to those industries in which low pay was a major factor.

Alongside action to extend the scope and powers of NEDC and the EDCs, parallel action could be taken to strengthen collective bargaining machinery to enable it to deal with matters relating to efficiency, manpower planning and related topics. The TUC has already adopted a policy which seeks to enable those industries covered by Wages Councils—which contain large concentrations of low paid workers—to develop along these lines. The implementation of this policy, coupled with the TUC policy for an extension of industrial democracy which would give workers, through their unions, a legally established right to become involved in the whole area of managerial decision making, would act as a continuing prod to employers who were lagging in their efforts to promote efficiency in order to meet the cost of a national minimum wage.

Training would be another area for much more positive action. The Tory Government, in response to pressure from employers who disliked direct intervention in their affairs, weakened the provisions of the Industrial Training Act. The introduction of a national minimum wage would provide the opportunity to put some real teeth into statutory obligations on employers to train low paid workers as part of a general programme of job restructuring and improved industrial efficiency, and the presence of union representatives on the training boards would help ensure employers met their obligations.

Some industries, faced with the need to install improved technology in order to raise efficiency at a time when their profits were being squeezed by the cost of meeting the national minimum wage, would require short-term financial assistance. There is no reason why the Government, as have both Labour and Tory Governments in the past, should not meet these needs by a system of development or investment loans which could be administered and controlled in conjunction with the NEDC and the EDCs. There would undoubtedly be a problem with those employers who, because of very high concentrations of low paid workers in their firms, the nature of their work, or their geographical location, would require high levels of financial aid spread over a long term. In such circumstances a system which combined loans with development grants and, where applicable, regional employment premiums, could be applied. Again, the EDCs could be used to establish the circumstances, confirm the need and monitor the results of such financial aid. Control of assistance from public funds would be further strengthened if, as previously suggested, an Industrial Democracy Act as proposed by the Labour Party in its election manifesto gave workers and their unions the legal right to intervene at the level of the enterprise where such assistance was being applied. Nor is there any reason why grants from public funds should not carry with them a direct element of public control with a body, such as the National Enterprise Board proposed by the Labour Party, taking over shares—or even the outright ownership—in firms which received grants.

What about the employer who, rather than face the difficulties created by the introduction of the national minimum wage, opted ruthlessly to cut back his labour force or to go out of business entirely and transfer his capital to an activity where there was the possibility of higher profits and fewer problems? For these characters more direct forms of sanction could be applied. For example, an alteration to the redundancy payments provisions could be constructed so that they carried loaded compensation related to discharges created by the introduction of the national minimum wage and were directly chargeable to the employer concerned; this would force the employer to face a very realistic economic choice between sacking workers and applying his mind and money to overcoming the problems with which he was confronted. Similarly, it should not be beyond the wit of a Labour Chancellor to devise a tax which penalized an employer who realized or transferred his capital in order to duck out of the responsibilities imposed on him by the introduction of the national minimum wage.

Those of our opponents who have not by this time recoiled in horror at the thought of such massive intervention by Government and unions in the affairs of industry will now pose their final questions: 'Where is the money coming from to finance these grants, loans, training schemes, price control mechanisms and the like? And who is going to meet the cost of ending low pay in the public services?' The answer, quite simply, is through redistribution of income and wealth.

In its 1974 election manifesto the Labour Party committed itself to a series of proposals which are well suited to fit into an overall programme to eliminate low pay. Its proposals on taxation, for example, can be structured so that high profit industries, property companies and the better off generally help to finance the changes needed to accommodate the introduction of the national minimum wage. Its proposals to take into public ownership profitable sections of industries or firms can again be related to the need to meet the cost of ending low pay. Why, for example, should not some of the very high profits which the pharmaceutical industry makes from the National Health Service be diverted to help pay decent wages to hospital workers? Related to a programme designed to eliminate low pay, the already existing proposals of the Labour Party would acquire a new sense of social purpose and one which would be readily understood by trade unionists on whose support the Labour Party depends.

In the past, articulate orthodox economists have exercised a disproportionate degree of influence within the Labour Movement. They have been able to play down the effectiveness of the national minimum wage as the major weapon to eliminate low pay because they have recognized that it would pose the need to introduce accompanying radical changes to curb the interaction of the market forces on which capitalism rests. We believe that the prevailing climate of opinion within the Labour Movement now creates an opportunity to negate those past influences and to change direction. The cumulative effect of post-war experience, particularly since the end of the first post-war Labour Government in 1950, has generated a new spirit within the Labour Movement which has recaptured the radical enthusiasm of the past in its desire to engineer fundamental changes in society. In this situation a policy of a national minimum wage can win wide acceptance within the Movement precisely because it will involve action to curb the market forces of capitalism and in the process give added justification and greater impetus to the direction in which the Labour Party must travel.

7. The Numbers Game

> I know a low paid worker when I see one, and I trust the trade union Movement to know a low paid worker better than anyone else.
>
> GEORGE WOODCOCK

It is not part of our function to attempt to identify every occupation which can be described as low paid by one definition or another or those industries in which low pay is a major factor and, on the basis of such identification, to quantify the problem by calculating the total number of low paid workers, deriving from that figure an estimate of the cost of introducing a national minimum wage. As we are not economists or statisticians we are not equipped to carry out such an exercise, but even if we were we would not attempt to do so. In the past others, apparently well qualified, have made many involved and elaborate excursions into the detailed arithmetic of low pay; the main result of the conflicting answers they have produced has been to perpetuate discussion about low pay without generating any corresponding determination to take action which will eliminate the problem.

There are a number of reasons for this. First, while in recent years a wealth of new information on low pay has become available it is still much too short on detail to justify any serious attempt at precise quantification; efforts in this direction therefore inevitably lead to frustrating indecision which demoralises those who want positive action but who find themselves continually trapped in discussions on points of detail which cannot be resolved while the broader policy implications become lost. Second, and equally important, the multi-dimensional nature of the solution we propose —a national minimum wage backed by wide ranging supportive action to introduce the radical economic and social changes necessary to make that national minimum wage a practical proposition—increases the difficulties of presenting a meaningful detailed statistical analysis at this stage.

Our concern is to establish the broad sweep of policies embracing the central principles which we believe to be essential to a political solution of the low pay problem. This imposes on us the requirement to make a logical presentation of our main arguments backed with sufficient detail to convince the Labour Movement that it should commit itself to the policies we advocate; when that act of commitment has been secured it will be for the specialists, statisticians and economists amongst them, to undertake the work of precise quantification and in the process to produce the kind of information which is still lacking.

Having said that, however, we recognize that we have reached a point where it is necessary to introduce some statistical evidence to underpin the views we have expressed so far and, more important, to give some indication of the problems involved so that our later consideration of the role and the responsibilities of the trade union Movement in a political solution to the low pay problem can be understood and appreciated by trade unionists themselves. In doing so, however, we are seeking to do no more than to sketch the broad outlines of the issues which will confront the Movement and to indicate the general direction in which it must travel and—bearing in mind that this book is intended for trade unionists—to do so with the minimum of detailed statistical analysis.

The largest single section of the employed labour force, numbering 7·9 million and accounting for 38 per cent of the total, consists of men, aged 21 and over, engaged on full-time manual work. It is therefore logical to begin an arithmetical examination of pay with this group.

The 1973 New Earnings Survey (NES)[1] showed that in April 1973 the average gross weekly earnings of this group, after discounting those whose pay was affected by absence, was £38·1 and the average weekly hours worked were 46·7. A breakdown of that average gross earnings figure shows that 16·3 per cent was derived from overtime payments; 9·6 per cent from payment by results schemes, bonuses, commission, etc.; 2·6 per cent from premium payments for shift or similar work and the remaining 71·5 per cent from all other payments, primarily basic wage rates.

These, however, are overall averages applying to nearly 8 million workers and a much more detailed breakdown is required before there can be any understanding of pay relationships. For example, 38·8 per cent of the men did not work overtime and this obviously affected their earnings in relation to the overall average. Further, 60·7 per cent did not receive PBR or similar payments and 81·6 per cent did not receive premium payments for shift or similar work. The extent to which these payments were spread amongst the labour force, and the extent to which the various payments overlapped, will affect the distribution of earnings and help to determine whether individual workers were high paid or low paid relative to the overall average earnings. In fact we know from the NES that half of the men received less than £36·60 and that 10 per cent received less than £24·60; Table 7.1 shows in greater detail how gross weekly earnings were distributed.

Table 7.1. Distribution of gross weekly earnings, full-time manual men, April, 1973

Percentage with weekly earnings less than					
£20	£25	£30	£35	£40	£50
2·2	10·8	25·7	43·9	62·0	85·9

We are now in a position where we can make some tentative judgements in order to pursue our examination. The TUC, at the 1973 annual Congress, adopted a policy which set £25 as the basic minimum wage for a standard work week. Clearly, most of the 10·8 per cent of the men whose gross earnings (including overtime, bonus payments, shift premiums, etc.) were below £25 were low paid by the TUC definition; just how many and by how much depends on how the earnings of the 850,000 men in this category were made up. It is at this point, unfortunately, that the information in the NES runs dry and further analysis must rely on pointing out likely areas and characteristics rather than presenting definite quantities.

A closer examination of the make-up of weekly earnings presented in the NES produces some useful clues in this direction; but before this examination is made it is necessary to define with greater precision the terms used in the NES to describe the various components of gross weekly earnings. They are as follows:

Overtime pay: the total sum paid, not merely the premium element, for all overtime hours worked. Thus, if four hours of overtime were paid at the rate of time-and-a-half it is the resulting six hours pay which is shown under this heading.

PBR etc. payments: all payments made under piecework and other payments by results schemes, bonuses, commission, profit sharing and any other incentive payments.

Shift etc. premiums: payments at higher rates for all shift work, night work or week-end work which is not treated as overtime. The amount shown under this heading is the premium element only and not the total pay for such periods of work.

All other pay: the remainder of gross weekly earnings after the components for overtime, PBR etc., shift etc. premiums have been deducted; it consists mainly of basic pay but can also include other elements such as pay for working in dirty or dangerous conditions, service pay, and an averaged out portion of London weighting allowances etc.

By isolating these various components it is possible to get some idea of how the average wage packet in different industries was made up and to gather some general impression of those workers who, despite additional payments from overtime or bonus schemes, could be described as low paid when reference is made to their basic rate. One way of doing this is to take the 27 main industrial groups (the Standard Industrial Classification presented in the NES)[2] and to isolate those in which the 'all other pay' component was less than the TUC target of £25 for the basic weekly minimum rate. These are shown in Table 7.2, which has been extended to include those main industrial groups in which the gross average earnings were less than the all industries and services average of £38·1 regardless of the level of 'all other pay'. In other words, two rudimentary tests have been applied to the 27 industries: whether 'all other pay' was below the TUC minimum basic wage target or whether the average earnings were below the all industries average, any industry meeting one or other, or both, of these criteria is included in the table.

Table 7.2. Make-up of average gross weekly earnings in selected industries (male manual workers)

	Total	*Over-time pay*	*PBR etc. pay-ments*	*Shift etc. premium pay-ments*	*All other pay*
	£	£	£	£	£
All industries and services	38·1	6·2	3·6	1·0	27·3
Group A					
Agriculture, forestry, fishing	29·5	3·7	1·7	0·1	24·0
Textiles	35·2	5·1	4·8	1·2	24·1
Clothing and footwear	33·3	2·7	6·1	0·1	24·4
Professional and scientific services	30·2	4·0	1·0	0·9	24·2
Miscellaneous services	30·3	3·7	1·6	0·3	24·8
Public administration	31·1	4·3	2·7	0·3	23·8
Group B					
Bricks, pottery, glass, cement etc.	40·3	7·6	6·6	1·4	24·7
Group C					
Distributive trades	32·2	4·6	1·9	0·3	25·4
Insurance, banking, finance and business services	33·1	4·1	0·8	0·4	27·8
Instrument engineering	36·2	5·3	2·5	0·4	27·9

It will be seen that in the majority of cases, six out of the total of ten industries which meet the criteria, the pay can be said to be low by both tests and for convenience of reference these have been presented together as Group A in the table. In one industry (shown as Group B) 'all other pay' is below £25 but average gross earnings are above the all industries average. In the remaining three (shown as Group C) the 'all other pay' component is above £25 but the average gross earnings are below £38·1. Thus, while some common tendencies have emerged there is sufficient deviation to merit a closer study.

Taking the six industries in Group A it can be seen that while the gap between their 'all other pay' component and the average of that component for all industries and services ranged from £2·5 to £3·5 the gap at the other end of the table, total gross earnings, was wider and ranged between £2·9 and £8·6. Nor does there appear to be much consistency in the relationships between 'all other pay' and gross earnings. In the textiles industry, for example, 'all other pay' was £3·2 below the all industries level yet on gross earnings the difference with all industries had narrowed to £2·9. On the other hand agriculture, forestry and fishing, which with an 'all other pay' component of £3·3 was only marginally worse off than textiles, had a difference of £8·6 with all industries on gross earnings. Obviously, it is the components between 'all other pay' and total earnings, and particularly the overtime and PBR payments, which have introduced variations of this kind.

In the make-up of average gross earnings in all industries and services the overtime pay component contributed £6·2 (16·3 per cent) of the total. In not one of the six industries in Group A did overtime pay make such a large contribution, either in monetary or in percentage terms. In all but two of the industries in Group A (textiles and clothing and footwear) the contribution of PBR etc. payments was less than in the all industries average, where it accounted for 9·6 per cent of total earnings and produced £3·6. Similarly, except in the case of textiles and professional and scientific services, the shift etc. premium payments did not generate—in money or percentage terms—the all industries average.

However, we are still considering averages and—as when dealing with the total male manual workforce earlier—the extent to which the earnings derived from overtime and payments by results were spread amongst the labour force will be an important factor in determining individual earnings levels, particularly when the industry can be defined as low paid overall. Table 7.3 contains the six industries in Group A and shows the proportions of the workforce who received various payment components.

It can be seen that the proportion of the men in the six industries working overtime was much lower than the all industries average and this in part explains why the average amount produced by overtime earnings in each one of the six industries was below the all industries average. But it is only a partial explanation of the situation. If we take, for example, the overtime earnings in the industry in Group A where the average earnings from overtime were the lowest (clothing and footwear) and compare it with the all industries average we find that the all industries average payment

Table 7.3. Proportion of male manual workers in selected industries who received particular payments

	Percentage of workers who received:		
	Overtime pay	*PBR etc. payments*	*Shift etc. premiums*
All industries and services	61·2	39·3	18·4
Agriculture, forestry, fishing	50·9	13·6	1·2
Textiles	58·9	41·6	25·6
Clothing and footwear	39·7	29·9	2·5
Professional and scientific workers	51·7	24·9	21·8
Miscellaneous services	46·6	18·3	4·8
Public administration	53·5	49·2	9·3

was 130 per cent higher. If, however, we compare the average amount received by those workers who actually received overtime payments we find the following: all industries and services £10·2, clothing and footwear £6·8, a difference of only 50 per cent. Thus the smaller proportion of men in clothing and footwear receiving overtime pay has narrowed the real difference in payments to those actually working overtime. The full effects of this can be seen in Table 7.4.

Coupling this information with that in Tables 7.2 and 7.3 we can now make some general conclusions about overtime pay as it affects workers in the six industries in Group A. First, it accounted for a much smaller proportion of the total average earnings in those industries than in the average for all industries. Second, fewer men in those six industries worked overtime than in all industries and services. Third, the overtime hours of those men in the six industries who actually worked overtime were not markedly below those of men in all industries who worked overtime; although the average hourly rate of overtime pay in those six industries was considerably below that of all industries. Finally, we can conclude that these factors will influence the distribution of earnings in the six industries compared with the distribution in all industries.

Consideration of the earnings generated by PBR etc. payments introduces variations of some complexity. In two of the industries in Group A (clothing and footwear and textiles) PBR etc. payments exceeded the average for all industries and in two industries (textiles and public administration) the proportion of workers receiving such payments was greater than in all industries. However these facts, presented in Tables 7.2 and 7.3, mask the extent to which in some industries there is a marked distinction between what are traditionally called pieceworkers and time workers; which can result in several widely differing wage structures existing within an industry. The effects of this can be seen in Table 7.5 which shows the make-up of earnings of men who actually received PBR etc. payments.

Table 7.4. Overtime hours and overtime pay of employees who received overtime pay

	Overtime hours	*Overtime pay* £	*Overtime pay per hour* £
All industries and services	10·5	10·2	0·97
Agriculture, forestry, fishing	9·5	7·2	0·76
Textiles	10·0	8·6	0·86
Clothing and footwear	7·6	6·8	0·88
Professional and scientific services	9·1	7·8	0·86
Miscellaneous services	9·4	7·9	0·84
Public administration	9·5	8·1	0·85

If agriculture, forestry, fishing is excluded (where the relatively small non-agricultural element, such as the cash payment on catch in fishing, distorts the overall picture) it can be seen that the resulting pattern tends to indicate those industries (such as textiles and clothing and footwear) where there is a clear distinction between pieceworkers and time workers; those (such as miscellaneous services) where a section of the labour force receives commission and bonus on sales etc.; and those (such as public administration and professional and scientific services, which includes manual workers in the educational and medical and dental services) where there has been a recent if uneven spread of incentive payments schemes. These distinctions are most clearly reflected in the extent

Table 7.5. Make-up of average gross weekly earnings of male manual workers who received PBR etc. payments

	Total	*Overtime pay*	*PBR etc. pay-ments*	*Shift etc. premiums*	*All other pay*
	£	£	£	£	£
All industries and services	40·3	6·1	9·3	1·2	23·8
Agriculture, forestry, fishing	32·4	3·3	12·6	0·0	16·5
Textiles	37·2	5·4	11·6	1·8	18·4
Clothing and footwear	36·5	2·2	20·3	0·1	13·9
Professional and scientific services	34·5	5·0	4·0	1·1	24·4
Miscellaneous services	35·1	3·1	8·9	0·5	22·5
Public administration	32·9	3·9	5·4	0·3	23·3

to which PBR etc. payments contributed to the gross earnings of those who actually received such payments.

The initial conclusion that must be drawn from these figures is that the mere inclusion of an element of PBR etc. payment in the average earnings of workers in the six industries does not necessarily indicate that such a payment is making any significant contribution to overcoming the problem of low earnings in an even fashion throughout the industry. If there is a sharp distinction between pieceworkers and time workers within an industry; or if the earnings from PBR etc. schemes are not evenly distributed amongst the labour force, or if there is an overlap, as Table 7.5 would seem to indicate, between overtime payments and PBR etc. payments so that both are concentrated on very much the same group of workers, this will affect the distribution of earnings and produce concentrations of low paid workers in industries that are low paid overall.

This can be seen from Table 7.6, which gives the distribution of earnings in the six industries under consideration. It shows for example that, despite the fact that the PBR etc. payment component in the make-up of earnings in the textiles and clothing and footwear industries was much larger than the all industries average, the proportion of workers with gross earnings below £25 a week was higher in those two industries than in all industries.

Table 7.6. Distribution of gross weekly earnings (male manual workers)

	Percentage with weekly earnings less than:						
	£20	£25	£30	£35	£40	£50	£80
All industries and services	2·2	10·8	25·7	43·9	62·0	85·9	99·3
Agriculture, forestry, fishing	6·5	38·5	63·1	80·7	89·4	96·0	99·4
Textiles	3·4	14·6	30·7	51·1	72·0	92·3	99·8
Clothing and footwear	5·1	19·6	38·9	60·3	79·3	94·9	100·0
Professional and scientific services	7·8	33·4	56·7	76·1	86·3	96·0	99·8
Miscellaneous services	13·4	31·8	55·5	73·3	84·4	94·9	99·5
Public administration	2·6	26·3	52·9	73·0	86·1	96·6	99·9

So far we have only considered six of the ten industries included in Table 7.2 and before an attempt can be made to draw general conclusions it is necessary to examine in closer detail the remaining four industries; those in Groups B and C.

The only industry in which the 'all other pay' component was below £25 and the gross earnings were above the all industries average of £38·1 was bricks, pottery, glass, cement etc. As can be seen from Table 7.2, payments in this industry for overtime, PBR etc. and shift premiums were above the all industries average. The proportion of workers receiving these payments was also above the all industries average: 70·3 per cent received overtime pay, 58·1 received PBR etc. payments and 23·4 per cent received shift etc. premiums. These higher than the all industries average figures meant that there was a much more even spread of payments derived from these various components of gross earnings and this was reflected in the distribution of earnings, as shown in Table 7.7.

Thus, although the bricks, pottery, glass, cement etc. industry had an 'all other pay' component £2·6 below the all industries average, the average gross earnings were £2·2 above those of all industries because of the level of additional payments for overtime, PBR etc. and shift premiums. This, coupled with the wider spread of those additional payments over the labour force, a feature in part conditioned by the continuous nature of the productive process in the industry, had a significant effect on earnings of the lowest paid workers.

In the three industries where the 'all other pay' component was

Table 7.7. Distribution of gross weekly earnings in bricks, pottery, glass, cement etc. industry (male manual workers)

Percentage with weekly earnings less than:						
£20	£25	£30	£35	£40	£50	£80
1·2	5·1	16·6	33·9	53·7	82·2	99·4

Table 7.8. Proportion of male manual workers in selected industries who received particular payment

	Percentage of workers who received:		
	Overtime pay	*PBR etc. payments*	*Shift etc. premium payment*
Distributive trades	52·6	24·2	5·7
Insurance, banking, finance and business services	44·0	9·6	4·1
Instrument engineering	67·2	31·5	7·2

above £25 but the gross weekly earnings were below the all industries average (Group C, Table 7.2) in one case, distributive trades, 'all other pay' was £1.90 below the all industries average while in insurance, banking, finance and business services it was £0·5 above and in instrument engineering it was £0·6 above. However, as with Group A, the contribution made by overtime, PBR and shift premium payments to total earnings in the three industries was lower than the all industries average; but, as shown in Table 7.8, there was a considerable difference in the three industries in the proportions of the workers who actually received these payments.

As is to be expected, the variations shown in Table 7.8 coupled with the average amounts of the payments for the particular components of gross earnings were reflected in the distribution of those payments to the workforce. Table 7.9 shows the average overtime

Table 7.9. Overtime hours and overtime pay of employees who received overtime pay (male manual workers)

	Overtime hours	*Overtime pay*	*Overtime pay per hour*
		£	£
Distributive trades	10·0	8·8	0·88
Insurance, banking, finance and business services	9·6	9·3	0·97
Instrument engineering	8·2	7·9	0·96

Table 7.10. Make-up of average gross weekly earnings of male manual workers who received PBR etc. payments

	Total	*Over-time pay*	*PBR etc pay-ments*	*Shift etc. pre-miums*	*All other pay*	*PBR etc. payments on percentage of average earnings less overtime*
	£	£	£	£	£	%
Distributive trades	37·0	5·4	7·7	0·4	23·5	24·5
*Insurance, banking, finance and business services	—	—	—	—	—	—
Instrument engineering	38·8	4·9	8·1	0·9	25·0	23·8

* For statistical reasons details not published, but (as shown in Tables 7.2 and 7.8) the overall average PBR etc. payment was £0·8 while 9·6 per cent of the work force actually received such payments; it can therefore be estimated that the average amount received by those who received PBR etc. payments was £8·3.

hours and payments of those men who actually worked overtime, while Table 7.10 shows the make-up of pay of those who received

PBR etc. payments. Finally, to round off the picture, Table 7.11 gives the distribution of earnings in the three industries and, as to be expected from information in the previous tables, shows that instrument engineering presented a more favourable picture than the other two industries.

We are now in a position to make some general observations about pay in all of the ten industries which have been examined.

The one factor to emerge quite clearly is the importance of overtime payments in raising the levels of total earnings. Except in one

Table 7.11. Distribution of gross weekly earnings (male manual workers)

	Percentage with earnings less than:						
	£20	£25	£30	£35	£40	£50	£80
Distributive trades	7·2	26·1	47·6	66·9	80·3	94·5	99·7
Insurance, banking, finance and business services	9·6	29·2	48·3	63·4	75·5	92·0	99·4
Instrument engineering	0·8	9·0	26·9	50·5	70·3	94·1	99·2

industry (clothing and footwear) overtime pay was a much larger component of gross earnings, in both monetary and percentage terms, than PBR etc. payments. On the other hand, however, in only one industry (bricks, pottery, glass, cement, etc.) did the level of overtime pay exceed the all industries average; and this was the only industry of the ten in which gross average earnings exceeded those of all industries. The importance of overtime pay becomes more apparent as the examination is carried deeper. Not only were average overtime earnings less in nine of the ten industries than in all industries, but in the same nine a smaller proportion of the labour force actually worked overtime and amongst that proportion the overtime pay per hour was less, often appreciably so, than the all industries figure.

To grasp the real significance of these facts it must be recalled that in all industries and services average overtime pay accounted for more than 16 per cent of the average earnings and for the 61 per cent of the men who actually worked overtime their average 10·5 hours a week put an additional £10·2 in their pay packets. The often quoted average of 46·7 hours a week for male manual workers therefore obscures the fact that four out of every ten men do not work overtime and the six that do have an average week of more than 50 hours. In short, much of the cash in workers' pay packets gets there through overtime working and because—for one reason or another—that overtime is not evenly spread amongst the work-force a large number of workers are low paid in terms of average earnings.

Because overtime has become such an important component of total earnings, workers who are on low basic rates and have less than the average opportunity to work overtime suffer an additional disability: what overtime they do work adds less than a similar amount of overtime does to a worker on a higher basic rate, precisely because overtime pay is a function of basic rates. Tables 7.4 and 7.9 show the effects of this on the average rates of overtime pay per hour of overtime worked and demonstrate how a worker in miscellaneous services, for example, receives less than 87 per cent of the all industries average hourly rate for overtime work.

It is less easy to draw general conclusions from the effects of PBR etc. payments in the ten industries, but nonetheless some tendencies do emerge. In three of the ten industries PBR etc. payments, in both monetary and percentage terms, accounted for a greater part of gross earnings than in the all industries average. In two of these (textiles and clothing and footwear) there is a traditional division between pieceworkers and dayworkers, which we have already mentioned, and in the third (bricks, pottery, cement, glass) the continuous nature of the process lends itself to PBR etc. systems and a high proportion of the labour force is engaged on them. In the remaining seven industries the contribution of PBR etc. payments to gross earnings was less than in the all industries average and except in one instance (public administration) they were received by a smaller proportion of the workforce; a somewhat similar pattern to that of overtime payments.

One fact which does stand out, and it is again related to overtime, is the extent to which there was an appreciable overlap between PBR etc. payments and overtime, as shown in Tables 7.5 and 7.10. Reference to those tables shows that in three of the industries the amount of overtime pay received by men who also received PBR etc. payments was greater than the average overtime pay for that industry and in every other case it was only slightly less. (It will also be noted from those tables that the workers receiving PBR etc. payments received either the average or more than the average shift etc. premium payments for the industry, indicating another area of overlap.) It would appear, therefore, that the highest paid workers in those industries, as shown up in the distribution of earnings tables, are those who add to their basic rate by a combination of overtime, PBR etc. payments and shift etc. premium payments and that it is the narrow dispersion of these payments that accounts for the large proportion of low paid workers in most of those industries.

From this point it would be easy to argue, as many have, that the obvious way to improve the position of the low paid is to concentrate on total earnings rather than on basic rates and to direct efforts towards providing low paid workers with additional earnings opportunities, primarily through schemes designed to improve labour efficiency and to relate earnings to that improved efficiency. The proponents of such methods state that they are better suited to the varied and complex wage structures which exist throughout industry, and that, unlike additions to basic rates, they would cause the minimum disturbance to existing internal differentials in industries.

There are a number of weaknesses in this argument. The main one is that it overlooks the relatively limited contribution which output related payments, PBR etc. schemes, make to average gross earnings in industry generally; accounting for less than 10 per cent of average earnings and being an element in the pay packets of less than 40 per cent of male manual workers. To extend such schemes to make any appreciable difference in the earnings of, for example, the lowest paid 10 per cent of the male manual workers with gross earnings of less than £24·6 a week would demand an ingenuity not yet displayed by negotiators and, moreover, would undoubtedly require the kind of modifications in wage structures and bargaining arrangements which the advocates of such methods seek to avoid.

To argue that low pay can be solved by methods which concentrate on improved utilization of labour is a popular course of action in an inflationary situation and one which will find a sympathetic ear, if nothing else, from economists. It was for this reason, as we have already seen, that the National Board for Prices and Incomes considered low pay only as a detailed aspect of its major objective to raise productivity; it was an attitude which left a deep impression and which has conditioned the minds of many of those who have subsequently studied the problem. It has yet to be proved, however, that this single minded approach of the NBPI can solve the problem.

An example of the inadequacy of the NBPI policy can be demonstrated by the experiences of local authority manual workers. It will be recalled that in March 1967 the NBPI reported that the local authorities' services contained large concentrations of workers whose earnings were amongst the lowest in the country; rejecting a general increase in wage rates as the solution, the NBPI recommended that the solution should be found in schemes 'that will directly relate pay to improved productivity.' The report noted that in October 1966 approximately 7½ per cent of local authority manual workers were covered by incentive bonus schemes and, on a break-down of earnings, that incentive payments accounted for some 3 per cent of gross average earnings. Considerable efforts, owing much more to the determination of the unions than to the enthusiasm of the employers, were made to implement this recommendation. The results can be gathered from the NES which showed, in April 1973, that PBR etc. schemes had been extended to cover 55 per cent of local authority male manual workers and the element of PBR etc. payments contributed 9·5 per cent to their average gross earnings. On the surface this looks like a success story, but there is another side to it. Between October 1966 and April 1973, the average gross hourly earnings of male local authority manual workers rose by 81 per cent; over the same period the average gross hourly earnings of male manual workers in all industries rose by 84 per cent. In October 1966, the average gross hourly earnings of local authority manual workers were 55 per cent of the all industries average; in April 1973 the figure was 54 per cent. Thus, after more than five years of considerable effort in the direction recommended by the NBPI, the position of the local authority manual workers relative to all industries was marginally worse; had it not been for the six week 'dirty job' strike in 1970, which made a considerable addition to basic rates, the position of local authority workers would have shown a continuing deterioration.

It may be protested that local authority manual workers are but one example, that they are not necessarily typical of low paid workers and that their experience cannot be transferred to a wider setting. We hold a contrary view. Many low paid workers are to be found in the service industries; or among those workers performing 'service' functions in industries where many process workers are employed on piecework or some other incentive schemes; or in industries such as agriculture where traditional PBR schemes are difficult, if not impossible, to apply. All of these workers therefore have many common characteristics with local authority manual workers.

How, then, have incentive schemes been applied to local authority workers? The overwhelming majority are work-studied incentive schemes operated within a nationally negotiated framework which is then applied, through further local negotiations, to meet the specific situations at local level. This type of incentive scheme, or variants which ultimately rely on the sharing by workers in savings in labour costs, are the kind which it has been proved can be applied to 'service' or non-process workers and, provided they are strictly controlled by unions, can be made to operate to the benefit of the workers. They have one distinct disadvantage: they are all related to the basic rate. If the basic rate is low the additional earnings generated by the incentive scheme are correspondingly low. An indication of the consequences of this situation is to be found in the fact that, in April 1973, the average incentive bonus payment to the local authority manual workers who actually received such payments was £5·3, compared with £9·3 in all industries and services and £10·7 in manufacturing industries. Further evidence is to be found in the fact that of the 39 national agreements covering manual workers receiving PBR etc. payments listed in the NES in only ten was the PBR etc. payment lower than in local government. Eight of that ten were also in the public services (public transport, water supply, health) and the other two (retail co-operatives and company owned road passenger transport) were service industries.

To advocate productivity or efficiency related earnings as the major contribution to the solution of low pay, therefore, glosses over a number of important factors.

First, it ignores the fact that even in manufacturing industries, PBR etc. payments apply to only a minority of the workforce and make a relatively small contribution to gross average earnings. To attempt to apply such payments at the level and over the area needed to make any real improvement to the earnings of low paid workers would not only require a major restructuring of existing wages systems, it would also place low paid workers in a disadvantageous position relative to the rest of the workforce, in that they would need to place a disproportionate reliance on PBR etc. payments to raise and maintain the level of their earnings.

Second, it overlooks that the service-based nature of much low paid work requires the application of work studies and similar schemes which produce extra earnings as a function of basic wage rates. Therefore, when basic rates are set low the additional earnings generated by the scheme are correspondingly low. This, coupled with the situation outlined in the preceding paragraph, will compound the disadvantageous position of low paid workers.

Third, it ignores the practical difficulties in applying such schemes, even those which are most suitable, to service industries and occupations. Considerable resources of technical know-how are required, and not least a substantial body of trained specialists who can tailor the schemes to meet the wide variety of circumstances found in service-based work situations. Management resistance can add considerably to the difficulties. The introduction of work study officers, management services specialists, etc., is frequently taken by many managers to imply a lack of confidence in their managerial abilities and to represent a threat to their power; they react by becoming obstructionists. The combined result of these two factors is to slow down the rate of introduction of schemes, which is a long-term project even in the best of circumstances, and to limit their application to those jobs where the minimum of effort is required to apply the schemes.

None of the problems outlined above are insoluble, but their solution does require them to be placed within the context of an overall policy to eliminate low pay and which has as its catalyst the establishment of a national minimum wage.

Such a policy would undoubtedly pose the need for a revision and re-negotiation of wage structures over a wide area. Unions and managements would, for example, need to give careful consideration to the relationships between basic rates and PBR etc. payments in the light of the level of the national minimum wage. For its part, management would have to examine the economics of overtime pay when set against the additional output it produces and the extent to which overtime is really justified as distinct from being a device to increase earnings and attract labour. Unions would have to consider the same problem on the basis of securing realistic basic rates and the minimum amount of necessary overtime. In service-based low pay industries this kind of exercise would present unions with the opportunity to construct productivity-efficiency payment schemes in which the additional earnings generated had an acceptable relationship to both basic rates and gross earning. Employers in low paid industries, faced with the need to meet the national minimum wage as their initial labour cost, would have a sharp spur on their flanks to urge them forward in negotiations with unions in an endeavour to improve efficiency in ways which the unions found acceptable.

Many of these objectives, particularly the overall need to make a reassessment of the relative values of the various components of total earnings, are desirable in themselves; but without a specific commitment to a definite central objective—which we believe is possible by the adoption of a planned programme to eliminate low pay within the setting of the proposals for political action which we made in the previous chapter—it is extremely unlikely that the trade union Movement could be persuaded to embark on such an exercise. Even given that commitment the task before the unions will be of considerable magnitude and one which will challenge many well established concepts and practices. Nonetheless, we are convinced that the challenge must be made and met if low pay is to be eliminated and if low paid workers are to be given a demonstration of the ability of the trade union Movement to act in their interests.

8. Women and White Collars

> There have been instances, because of the lack of training facilities, because of the lack of transferability in entitlements, because of lack of movement from one place to another, where some have come off worse than others.
>
> FRANK COUSINS

In the previous chapter, we confined our statistical examination to the earnings of men manual workers but obviously any study of low pay would be incomplete without consideration of the two other categories which go to make up the labour force and which, because of widely differing circumstances, require separate examination: men non-manual workers and women workers, both manual and non-manual. In this chapter, therefore, we will look at these two categories and attempt on the basis of readily available statistical evidence to isolate the major characteristics which must be taken into account when formulating a policy designed to eliminate low pay.

Full-time men non-manual workers are the second largest group in the employed labour force: they number 4·2 million and account for 20 per cent of the total. The first characteristic that stands out is that, in relation to men manual workers, their earnings are much higher but their average working week is much less. The 1973 NES showed that their gross average weekly earnings, excluding those whose pay was affected by absence, were £48·1, some 20 per cent higher than those of manual workers, while their average weekly hours were 38·8, nearly eight hours less.

On the basis of these figures alone it is already apparent that there will be important differences in the make-up of average earnings between manual and non-manual men and that these are likely to affect the distribution of earnings and the relative proportion of non-manual men who can be described as low paid.

As can be seen in Table 8.1, overtime pay was a much less important component in the earnings of non-manual men than in the earnings of manual men. This, coupled with the average weekly

Table 8.1. Make-up of average gross weekly earnings, full-time non-manual men

		Percentage of total
	£	%
Total	48·1	
Overtime pay	1·4	3·0
PBR etc. payments	1·3	2·8
Shift etc. premium payments	0·2	0·4
All other pay	45·2	93·8

hours of the non-manual men, had obvious repercussions on the relative average gross hourly earnings. Whereas for manual men the average earnings went down from 81·7p an hour to 79·2p an hour when overtime hours and earnings were excluded, for non-manual men it went up marginally from 121·6p to 121·7p an hour. Expressed in a different fashion, we can say that while the average weekly earnings of non-manual men were 20 per cent higher than those of manual men their average hourly earnings including overtime were 49 per cent higher and excluding overtime they were 54 per cent higher. Thus the reliance which manual men have on overtime earnings to maintain their pay levels does not apply to non-manual men.

The other two specified components of average weekly earnings, PBR etc. payments and shift etc. premium payments, were also much less important to non-manual men and, as shown in Table 8.2, the proportion of non-manual men receiving any of these specified components was much smaller than was the case with manual men.

The total effect of this differing composition of average weekly earnings and the smaller proportion of the workforce receiving specified payments makes it much easier to identify those groups of non-manual men who can be described as low paid by reference to the TUC policy of £25 basic rate for a standard working week. With the 'all other pay' component accounting for 93·8 per cent of total earnings and with overtime, PBR and shift payments distributed so narrowly, the number of workers with gross weekly earnings above £25 who had a basic rate lower than that figure will

Table 8.2. Proportion of non-manual men who received particular payments

	%
Overtime pay	18·9
PBR etc. payments	7·9
Shift etc. premium payments	3·9

be relatively small. A straight-forward examination of the distribution of earnings will therefore provide a positive indication of those industries where low paid non-manual men are likely to be found on the basis of the TUC formula.

It will be seen from Table 8.3 (presented on the basis of the Standard Industry Classification in the NES) that the distribution of earnings clearly indicates those industries where the highest proportion of low paid non-manual men are to be found. If the all industries and services average of 7·4 per cent with weekly earnings less than £25 is taken as an initial reference point there are seven industries in which a higher percentage is to be found; it will not come as a surprise that six of these industries also featured in the area of low pay when manual men were considered in the previous chapter. In all but two of the six industries (professional and scientific services and public administration) PBR etc. payments to non-manual men accounted for a higher percentage of total earnings than in the all industries average and a higher proportion of the labour force in those industries received them; so the possibility of a man in one of those industries with earnings of less than £25 receiving a basic rate below that figure was correspondingly greater.

We are left, then, with the clear conclusion that the most direct and effective method of dealing with low pay amongst non-manual workers is to increase basic wage rates, which fits in admirably with our strategy. This does not mean, however, that there are no complicating factors. Many non-manual men are on incremental

Table 8.3. Distribution of gross weekly earnings, non-manual men

	Percentage with weekly earnings less than						
	£20	£25	£30	£35	£40	£50	£80
All industries and services	2·1	7·4	17·8	30·4	42·8	65·6	92·5
Agriculture, forestry, fishing	3·5	11·2	23·1	40·6	51·8	67·1	89·5
Mining and quarrying	0·3	1·9	10·8	26·0	37·7	64·2	94·0
Food, drink and tobacco	0·8	6·4	19·1	34·7	47·9	70·8	92·5
Chemicals and allied industries	0·5	3·6	9·7	19·4	31·7	57·0	89·6
Metal manufacture	0·2	3·8	15·3	30·3	46·9	73·5	95·2
Mechanical engineering	0·8	4·5	14·4	29·5	45·8	72·4	94·5
Instrument engineering	0·4	3·0	10·2	23·8	42·3	72·8	96·2
Electrical engineering	0·4	2·2	8·6	20·0	34·4	64·1	92·5
Shipbuilding and marine engineering	0·0	4·0	11·9	22·6	37·3	72·9	96·6
Vehicles	0·4	2·3	7·8	18·2	31·2	61·2	93·7
Metal goods not elsewhere specified	1·1	4·6	13·7	28·2	44·4	69·2	94·0
Textiles	1·9	5·2	13·0	28·3	43·4	65·1	89·6
Clothing and footwear	3·9	14·0	25·1	36·3	51·4	75·4	91·1
Bricks, pottery, cement, glass etc.	1·0	4·4	12·3	25·0	40·8	65·2	94·0
Timber, furniture etc.	2·3	10·1	19·1	35·8	48·6	73·2	95·3
Paper, printing and publishing	1·6	5·4	13·2	23·8	35·2	59·6	90·2
Other manufacturing industries	1·8	4·1	10·5	25·2	42·7	68·1	92·4
Construction	1·3	4·6	11·9	22·8	36·8	63·7	93·7
Gas, electricity, water	1·0	3·9	14·7	25·9	40·4	63·7	94·9
Transport and communication	1·2	4·4	13·6	27·1	40·4	63·2	92·8
Distributive trades	4·7	18·3	37·4	53·2	64·6	79·4	94·1
Insurance, banking, finance and business services	2·4	7·2	16·9	28·2	38·6	57·7	86·5
Professional and scientific services	3·4	8·0	16·3	27·3	37·3	58·8	92·5
Miscellaneous services	4·4	13·5	29·5	45·5	58·7	73·5	93·5
Public administration	2·0	7·9	19·3	30·7	41·9	66·4	93·0

salary scales; in these cases low pay is a transitory feature of working life, lasting only while sufficient length of service, experience or qualifications are accumulated to progress up the salary scale beyond the point which can be defined as marking the level of low pay. To act on the basic rate to improve the position of the low paid by means of a national minimum wage will affect the lower points of the salary scales and will present unions with the need to re-think their attitudes towards the length of the scales, the steps in them and the pay relationship between those on the lowest points and those on the higher points. In some non-manual occupations there will also be the need, as in the case of some manual occupations, for unions to redefine the relationship between basic rates and PBR etc. payments. The resolution of these difficulties should present no insurmountable problems given the fact that they are placed within the context of an overall trade union plan to eliminate low pay and, as in the case of the need to make somewhat similar revaluations for manual workers as noted in the previous chapter, are desirable trade union objectives in themselves.

The examination of low pay amongst non-manual men was a simple task; with women it becomes a much more complex operation of the need to make constant reference to the relationships of their pay to that of men, in order to indicate the factors which go to make up the difference in earnings as between men and women. Let us be quite clear, however, that the differences to which we refer will, in some instances, be economic manifestatons of the sex discrimination which exists in industry. The 1970 Equal Pay Act will, when it is fully implemented, go some way to removing that discrimination; but it will still leave a great deal to be accomplished before it can be claimed that there is no sex discrimination in the field of employment. A wider anti-discrimination law, of the kind currently under discussion in the Labour Movement, will take the process a step further; a national minimum wage—and the accompanying measures we advocate—can also make a positive contribution. When considering a policy to eliminate low pay, therefore, as far as women are concerned it must be seen as just one contribution to a much wider process.

There are 2 million women full-time manual workers in Britain, almost 10 per cent of the total adult employed labour force. Before making examination of their pay situation it is necessary to utter a few notes of caution insofar as the statistical material presented by the New Earnings Survey is concerned. First, there is an age problem. Whereas all of the NES data relating to men concerns those aged 21 and over, that relating to women concerns those aged 18 and over. Depending on the composition of the labour force in an industry, this age difference can lead to distortions when comparisons are made between the average earnings of men and women or of earnings distribution. Second, when the 1973 NES was carried out the earnings of 400,000 full-time manual women were affected by absence and as a result they are, in common with all other groups, excluded from most of the detailed presentation in the survey results. It must therefore be remembered that while little more than an eighth of the manual men were excluded on this basis for women the figure was a fifth, and this could have some influence, admittedly only small, on the results. Third, the NES definition of full-time is a worker normally expected to work for more than 30 hours a week (25 for teachers) excluding main meal breaks; a much greater proportion of full-time manual women than full-time manual men (77·6 per cent against 33·4 per cent) worked less than the 40 hours which most people normally associate with 'full-time' as applied to manual workers. This difference is not important when, for example, average hourly earnings are compared; but it needs to be borne in mind when average weekly earnings are compared, even if they exclude overtime. Finally, it must not be forgotten that NES data excludes part-time workers; in the case of manual men this means less than 2·5 per cent of the total but in the case of manual women it means 46 per cent of the total, and these are women about whose pay the NES has nothing to say.

The obvious starting point for an examination of the pay of manual women is to compare their position with that of their male counterparts; Table 8.4 shows the main relationships and in particular, because of the variation in average hours worked, how the difference between average earnings narrows somewhat when the comparison is made on an hourly rather than a weekly basis. The lesser importance of overtime pay to women workers, as displayed in the table, has its reflection in the components of the make-up of earnings, As Table 8.5 shows, overtime pay contributed only 3·8 per cent to

Table 8.4. Average gross weekly earnings, average hours and average gross hourly earnings; male and female manual workers

	Women	*Men*	*Women as percentage of men*
			%
Average gross weekly earnings, all industries and services	£19·7	£38·1	52
Average weekly hours	39·9	46·7	85
Average gross hourly earnings, including overtime pay and hours	49·6p	81·7p	61
Average gross hourly earnings, excluding overtime pay and hours	49·1p	79·2p	62

the average weekly earnings of manual women compared with 16·3 per cent for manual men, and a smaller proportion of the women actually worked overtime. This underlines the significance, noted in the previous chapter, which overtime work, or the absence of it, has assumed for manual workers and how it can be a major factor in determining whether a manual worker is high paid or low paid purely in terms of total earnings.

Table 8.5. Details of overtime pay and hours, men and women manual workers

	Women	*Men*
Average weekly overtime earnings	£0·8	£6·2
Average weekly overtime earnings as percentage average gross weekly earnings	3·8%	16·3%
Workers who received overtime pay		
percentage of workers	19·9%	61·2%
average overtime hours	5·7	10·5
average payment per week	£3·8	£10·2

With overtime making a relatively smaller contribution to their total earnings, PBR etc. payments played a much more important part in raising women's earnings above the basic rate. In percentage terms, as Table 8.6 shows, it consisted of a larger part of their average weekly earnings than with men and the proportion of women receiving such payments was only a little smaller than with the men, (in fact, if manufacturing industries alone are considered, 45·2 per cent of the manual women received PBR etc. payments against 43·3 per cent of the manual men).

Table 8.6. Details of PBR etc. payments, men and women manual workers

	Women	*Men*
Average weekly PBR etc. payments	£2·4	£3·6
PBR etc. payments as percentage of average gross weekly earnings	12·3%	9·6%
Workers who received PBR etc. payments		
percentage of workers	32·8%	39·3%
average payment	£7·4	£9·4

Given the level of average weekly earnings and the contribution made to those earnings by overtime and PBR etc. payments, it is not surprising that it is not possible to identify a single industry out of the 27 in the Standard Industrial Classification in which the 'all other pay' component for manual women was above the £25 level. Indeed, in only two (vehicles and public administration) was 'all other pay' above £19 whereas with manual men the lowest' all other pay' component (in public administration) was £23·8. This widespread low pay situation is clearly reflected in the distribution of earnings shown in Table 8.7 and where it can be seen that a number of the industries in the worse position are those (such as distribution, miscellaneous services, clothing and footwear) which have been met before when considering manual and non-manual men.

Summarizing the information we have presented on women manual workers, it can be said that the high incidence of low pay, both relative to men and in an absolute sense, was not due to any single factor but to a combination of factors. First, average basic pay was low as evidenced by the fact that the 'all other pay' component in the make-up of average weekly earnings at £16·3 was only 59 per cent of the same component for manual men. Second, the contribution of overtime to earnings was much less than in the case of men manual workers and, because of lower basic rates, what overtime was worked by manual women produced smaller returns than a similar amount of overtime for men; the average overtime pay of 67p an hour for women was only 69 per cent of the male average.

Table 8.7. Distribution of earnings of full-time manual women

	Percentage with weekly earnings less than:				
	£14	£18	£20	£25	£30
All industries and services	13·8	42·7	57·9	83·5	94·3
Food, drink and tobacco	6·5	29·0	45·5	79·9	93·4
Chemicals and allied industries	7·5	35·3	52·6	81·7	94·1
Metal manufacture	9·8	39·3	51·8	83·9	98·2
Mechanical engineering	7·5	27·5	39·8	74·3	93·4
Instrument engineering	7·0	31·6	45·6	86·6	97·1
Electrical engineering	3·8	24·3	40·4	79·6	95·3
Vehicles	3·0	13·8	25·0	51·3	80·2
Metal goods n.e.s.	12·0	40·7	56·3	86·6	97·4
Textiles	10·3	40·5	57·2	84·0	95·7
Clothing and footwear	14·1	50·0	66·2	88·1	95·8
Bricks, pottery, glass, cement etc.	12·5	43·8	57·2	82·7	93·3
Timber, furniture etc.	10·6	27·3	37·9	66·7	81·1
Paper, printing and publishing	6·9	27·9	48·7	81·1	93·3
Other manufacturing industries	9·7	38·3	55·4	85·7	95·7
Transport and communication	3·9	17·7	24·8	40·9	63·4
Distributive trades	26·9	65·4	76·3	91·5	98·4
Professional and scientific services	12·6	32·7	70·8	91·4	97·3
Miscellaneous services	34·9	65·3	76·2	89·9	96·4
Public administration	5·2	18·6	42·0	76·0	93·0

Third, although PBR etc. payments accounted for a greater proportion of the average weekly earnings of manual women and the percentage of them receiving such payments was only a little less than in the case of manual men, in monetary terms the average PBR etc. payment for women was only 67 per cent of the average payment made to men.

The combination of these factors produced a situation where, after excluding the effect of overtime pay and hours, 86·3 per cent of manual women were receiving average earnings of less than 62·5p which is equivalent to earnings (not basic rates) of £25 for a 40 hour week without overtime. Thus, without any doubt, women manual workers as a group contain an extremely large concentration of low paid workers and in certain industries, as indicated by the distribution of earnings in Table 8.7, there are women who are low paid even by the standards of manual women.

The other group of women, non-manual workers aged 18 and over, numbers 3·5 million and accounts for 17·5 per cent of the employed adult labour force. Their average gross weekly earnings of £24·7, in the 1973 NES, were a little more than half of those of their male counterparts and thus had approximately the same relationship as the weekly earnings of manual women to manual men. Their average weekly hours of 36·8 were 95 per cent of those of men non-manual workers, to make their average gross hourly earnings 55 per cent of those of men non-manual workers, a smaller proportion than in the case of manual women and men.

Table 8.8. Make-up of average weekly earnings of full-time non-manual women

		as percentage of total
	£	%
Total	24·7	
Overtime pay	0·3	1·2
PBR etc. payments	0·2	0·6
Shift etc. premium payments	0·1	0·6
All other pay	24·1	97·7

The make-up of the average gross weekly earnings of non-manual women, as can be seen in Table 8.8, was quite uncomplicated. Taken together average overtime pay, PBR etc. payments and shift etc. premium payments produced only £0·6 and accounted for only 2·4 per cent of the total weekly average earnings. Thus the 'all other pay' component of £24·1 accounted for a higher proportion (97·6 per cent) of average weekly earnings than in any of the groups of workers whose pay has been examined. The proportion of women non-manual workers receiving these specified payments was also the lowest of any of the groups that have been considered: 10·3 per cent received overtime pay, 3·3 per cent received PBR etc. payments and 6·3 per cent received shift etc. premiums. Thus with non-manual women the average weekly earnings were much closer to the basic weekly pay rate than with any other group of workers and the process of identifying those industries in which non-manual women were low paid in terms of basic rates can be accomplished by reference to the distribution of earnings as shown in Table 8.9.

Table 8.9. Distribution of earnings of full-time women non-manual workers

	Percentage with weekly earnings less than:				
	£14	£18	£20	£25	£30
All industries and services	7·5	26·9	38·2	61·7	78·2
Mining and quarrying	1·0	8·7	12·5	33·7	75·0
Food, drink and tobacco	8·8	32·2	46·2	74·2	87·9
Chemicals and allied industries	3·5	20·5	37·4	68·4	86·4
Metal manufacture	8·0	30·1	47·4	78·8	94·7
Mechanical engineering	6·3	31·5	52·9	83·9	94·5
Instrument engineering	5·8	31·4	49·6	76·9	90·1
Electrical engineering	2·2	12·9	34·4	74·1	92·2
Vehicles	2·7	16·0	29·9	69·4	87·1
Metal goods n.e.s.	7·8	32·8	50·7	82·4	93·0
Textiles	10·5	44·9	64·8	86·9	94·4
Clothing and footwear	8·0	38·0	55·5	83·0	92·0
Bricks, pottery, glass, cement etc.	11·2	34·9	56·6	85·5	95·4
Timber, furniture, etc.	8·2	35·3	62·3	85·3	96·7
Paper, printing and publishing	5·5	26·1	37·2	61·6	78·9
Other manufacturing industries	2·4	28·0	48·8	84·5	93·5
Construction	6·8	33·9	50·3	76·8	92·9
Gas, electricity, water	2·6	7·8	18·6	51·3	79·1
Transport and communication	4·4	17·4	23·5	53·1	73·4
Distributive trades	18·3	57·8	71·1	87·6	94·4
Insurance, banking, finance and business services	5·7	23·1	33·1	61·1	79·1
Professional and scientific services	4·5	16·5	24·1	41·9	60·7
Miscellaneous services	12·8	34·2	44·5	65·3	81·2
Public administration	2·8	11·4	23·3	53·5	77·4

After excluding the effect of overtime pay and hours, 56 per cent of non-manual women were receiving average earnings of less than 62·5p an hour, which is equivalent to earnings of £25 for a 40 hour week and given the very small contribution which PBR etc. payments and shift etc. premium made (a total of £0·3 a week to average earnings) this is a close indication of the basic pay situation of non-manual women.

In summary it can be said that although in quantitative terms the problem of low pay amongst women workers, both manual and non-manual, is greater than amongst men the nature of the solution remains the same; and it revolves around action to raise the basic rates of pay through a national minimum wage. As with the men, in some industries this will require accompanying negotiated changes; with women manual workers to establish a new relationship between basic rates and other components, particularly PBR etc. payments, of total earnings and with some women non-manual workers to restructure incremental salary scales. Progress in these directions, moving in step with similar action on men's wages, will repair many of the deficiencies in the Equal Pay Act which, while it has undoubtedly assisted in increasing the earnings of many workers can never by itself eliminate low pay amongst women workers.

9. The Grand Alliance

Tackling the low wage situation certainly demands government assistance; it demands socialist policies, but it is primarily a direct trade union job.

JACK JONES

To many people, certainly to a number of trade unionists, our insistence that low pay must be approached as a political issue and that the central feature of a policy designed to eliminate low pay must be a legally enforceable national minimum wage will be seen as a departure from what are claimed to be the traditional methods of British trade unionism, which emphasizes the direct collective bargaining process between unions and employers rather than state intervention. This, however, is not the case. In fact we can be pedantic and legitimately claim to be the traditionalists in this matter because a long standing clause in the TUC's constitution, which is included in every annual report, specifically states that one of the objectives of the TUC shall be to endeavour to establish 'a legal minimum wage for each industry or occupation.' Why, then, has the TUC failed to activate this principle in recent years as it has developed an increasing awareness of the need to develop a strategy against low pay? The answer is to be found in the way in which the trade union Movement responds to changes in the economic, political and social environment in which it operates and its marked tendency to adopt an empirical response to those changes; nowhere is this more apparent than in its attitude towards the involvement of the state in industrial affairs.

In the formative years following its establishment in 1868 the TUC was acutely aware of its own weakness and as a consequence it placed considerable reliance on the promotion of parliamentary activities to secure its objectives. To use the TUC's own words, it was 'a period in which the TUC's principal efforts were directed—with limited and intermittent success—towards influencing successive governments to protect the trade unions as societies, and to protect the worker as an individual human being'.[1] It is somewhat paradoxical that this period drew to a close after the 1906 general election, following the formation of the Labour Representation Committee and the return of 29 Labour MPs to the House of Commons, when trade unions began to establish a parliamentary base. Increasingly the TUC redirected its emphasis away from the political scene and eventually formalized this in 1920 when it abolished the Parliamentary Committee, which had acted as its pivotal point for fifty years, and replaced it with the General Council. This change was much more than mere semantics, it marked a new period in which the principal efforts of the TUC were to be directed towards industrial—not political—affairs. From time to time in the years that followed the TUC, as immediate circumstances dictated, devoted energy and attention towards realizing limited and specified objectives by political methods when it was realized that industrial methods were inadequate or inappropriate; but these were aberrations from the general trend of an attitude of mind which emphasized the self sufficency of trade unionism and placed increasing reliance on what became known as 'voluntary methods' as opposed to obligations imposed by law.

The growth of this tendency made a deep impression on the trade union Movement, and certainly on many of its leaders. It led ultimately to something approaching a separatist theory, which found its clearest recent expression in the memorandum[2] of evidence which the TUC General Council submitted to the Royal Commission on Trade Unions and Employers' Associations in 1966. In a section entitled 'The State and Trade Union Function' that memorandum said:

'It is where trade unions are not competent, and recognize that they are not competent, to perform a function, that they welcome the state playing a role in at least enforcing minimum standards, but in Britain this role is recognized as the second best alternative to the development by workpeople themselves of the organization, the competence, the representative capacity, to bargain and to achieve for themselves satisfactory terms and conditions of employment. In general, therefore, because this competence exists, the state stands aside, its attitude being one of abstention, of formal indifference.

'This general attitude of abstention on the part of the state arises, be it noted, from the competence of trade unions to safeguard the interests of their members. In other words, it is where this necessary protection is lacking that the state intervenes, because free collective bargaining is absent. Virtually all the traditional activities of the Ministry of Labour in the field of industrial relations can be described as complementary to free collective bargaining. . . . The difficult issues which arise regarding the role of the state concern the definition of what is complementary; in other words, which function trade unions would welcome the state performing and which functions if performed by the state would detract from the independence of the trade union Movement. Whether seeking legislation in a particular field is the most advantageous way for trade unions to proceed is a question which cannot be answered in the abstract. However, the considerations outlined above are relevant to every particular issue . . .'

In one very important sense the views expressed in the memorandum can be welcomed because they demonstrate a desire to avoid the dangers of corporate statism in which the trade union Movement becomes identified with, and absorbed in, the state machine and so ceases to be responsive to the desires and aspirations of its members, The memorandum does, however, have two weaknesses. First, it overlooks the extent to which the 'formal indifference' of the state exists only when such indifference benefits the employers and their political representatives. In other words, it fails to recognize that very often it is the incompetence, not the competence, of trade unions which enables the state to adopt a 'general attitude of abstention'. Second, an attitude which relegates the state to a passive role can limit the effectiveness of the trade union Movement by delaying necessary changes, or restricting their application, simply because it refuses to utilize trade union strength to pressurize the state into using its powers to bring those changes about. In other words, the 'voluntary methods' become a fetish which cannot be upset, even though effective alternative methods are available.

A classic example of how these two weaknesses can operate, and one which has a direct bearing on the problem of low pay, is the way in which the TUC tackled the problem of equal pay for women. From 1882 onwards, with almost monotonous regularity, delegates at the annual TUC passed resolutions in favour of equal pay but very little of a practical nature was done to implement these resolutions. In 1945 one of the first acts of the post-war Labour Government was to set up a Royal Commission on the subject and the TUC General Council duly submitted a detailed memorandum[3] of evidence in which, in a section entitled 'Three Lines of Advance', it set out its practical suggestions for implementing the principle of equal pay for equal work. First, it said, by pursuing a policy of full employment the Government would widen job opportunities for women and place them in a stronger position to demand higher rates of pay. Second, the Government could apply equal pay to its own employees, 'advise' local government to do the same and by recommendation 'influence' the decisions of those appointed to arbitration machinery and Wages Councils. Third, said the General Council, the securing of equal pay would 'depend to a considerable extent on further improvements in the trade union organization of women and the strengthening of their position in collective bargaining.' It concluded: 'It follows from what we have said that what is required for "equal pay for equal work" to be achieved in all industries and occupations is the speeding up of the developments already taking place in the levelling up of women's wages. Since such a policy would largely be effected through the established procedure of industrial negotiations and wage determination it can reasonably be supposed that no dislocating consequences would arise.'

Looking back it seems incredible that these were the limits of the General Council's proposals, in a lengthy memorandum, for a practical programme to introduce equal pay. Nowhere was there even a suggestion that direct legislative action by the Government should be used; instead the General Council placed its reliance on the traditional 'voluntary methods' which it believed could achieve results without dislocation.

This attitude prevailed in the TUC's discussions with successive post-war Governments on the question of equal pay. In 1963 an apparent shift of attitude occurred when the annual Congress carried a resolution which specifically called on the next Labour Government 'by legislative initiative' to secure equal pay throughout industry and commerce within a specified period. Yet six years later, with a Labour Government again in power, the TUC General Council was putting forward to Ministers a policy for the introduction of equal pay based on three points. First, a 'joint declaration of intent' by Government, CBI and TUC. Second, the application by Government of equal pay to industrial civil servants. Third, 'subsequent enabling legislation to give Government powers to bring into line employers who decline to co-operate on a voluntary basis.' This continuing emphasis on 'voluntary methods' by the TUC ended when, in September 1969, Employment Secretary, Barbara Castle announced to the Labour Party Conference that she would be introducing a Bill during the next session of Parliament which would provide for the full implementation of equal pay by the end of 1975.

At no specific point during the very long period during which the TUC had advocated equal pay did the General Council take a conscious decision that the focal point of the campaign should be switched from 'voluntary methods' to legislative action. Instead it moved, rather hesitantly by the standards of some trade unionists, from complete reliance on 'voluntary methods' to a position in 1969 where legislation would be used as a supportive action and then, when virtually confronted with a legislative initiative by Barbara Castle, to a subsequent position where it actually criticized the provisions of the Bill for not going far enough or fast enough—without apparently realizing that such a position was an admission that its previous policies had failed.

This brief case history of the trade union Movement's attitude towards equal pay illustrates very clearly the dangers inherent in an over-reliance on 'voluntary methods', and it has a number of parallels in the way in which the problem of low pay has been approached.

The most thorough-going examination of low pay occurred following the publication of the TUC General Council discussion document[4] in 1970 and its subsequent circulation to all affiliated unions for their comments and criticisms. In its summary of responses from unions the General Council drew the conclusion that there was general agreement among unions on the need for a policy to push up the wages of the lower paid, equally general agreement that this should be based primarily on the normal process of collective bargaining and that unions would welcome a TUC pronouncement on what could be considered a reasonable national minimum to pursue in negotiations. 'The majority of unions were not in favour of the Government introducing a statutory minimum before negotiators had had the chance of proving that they could do the job themselves within the context of union guidelines and the TUC's declaration,' said the General Council.

That the unions should reach this conclusion was hardly surprising, given the manner in which the General Council's discussion document presented the way in which a statutory national minimum wage would affect trade unions. The document noted that a major argument used against a statutory minimum wage was that it would inhibit the development of trade union organization amongst the low paid, and cited the Wages Councils industries as a case in point. It did add, however, that a 'partial' solution to this problem might be to introduce the statutory minimum in stages, giving employers an incentive to offset increased costs before the final deadline by proposing productivity and efficiency improvements and restructuring incomes and jobs. 'Workpeople who would be affected by such changes would in turn see the value of trade union membership as a way of protecting their interests and of obtaining standards above the minimum.'

But there was no similar attempt in the document to provide any possible solution to the next, and more fundamental, criticism it made of a legal minimum wage.

'However, a further and more important argument against a

statutory minimum is that the trade union Movement would in effect be inviting the state to intervene on a much bigger scale in the wage fixing process without having any prior assurance that a statutory minimum would in fact be introduced and thereafter maintained at a level anywhere near what would be acceptable. The fact that Governments have not given Wages Councils more positive objectives in their terms of reference lends support to the view that the state would take a restrictive view of its role in tackling the problem of low pay. On the contrary, Governments have shown a propensity to impose negative restraints on Wages Councils, notably in the context of incomes policy.'

One can imagine the effect of such an observation on trade unionists in 1970, at the end of a decade in which there had been constant conflict between unions and governments over what was popularly referred to as 'incomes policy' but which was in effect little more than wage restraint. It was inevitable, confronted in the TUC discussion document with the possibility of a situation arising in which the Movement would be further constrained by Government action, that unions would react by reasserting their belief in what they saw as the traditional 'voluntary methods' (this notwithstanding the fact that at the very same time they were in the process of discarding those 'voluntary methods' in favour of legislation as the method of securing equal pay for women workers).

In posing the issue in this way the TUC General Council encouraged those trade unionists who persist in an empirical approach —transferring an experience from one situation to another and completely different situation and clinging to attitudes created by a particular set of circumstances long after those circumstances have changed. The defeat, largely by trade union votes, of the NUPE resolution on a legal national minimum wage at the 1973 Labour Party Conference can be attributed in no small part to the way in which consideration of the TUC discussion document of 1970 helped to perpetuate out-dated attitudes in relation to low pay and the role of a Labour Government in a policy to eliminate low pay.

Ironically, the TUC General Council itself has shown signs that it recognizes that the reliance on 'voluntary methods' which has dominated central trade union strategy for so many years is an inappropriate approach to many modern industrial problems. In its memorandum of evidence to the Royal Commission on Trade Unions and Employers' Associations in 1966, from which we quoted earlier, it stated that the abstentionist role of government in industrial relations 'which has become traditional in Britain' still remained largely true. It then added, however: 'Yet a significant change has come about over the past five years, a change which is in the direction of statutory intervention. In brief this change can be seen to arise from what may be termed an overall Government view of labour market policy as a key element in its economic policy. This is not so much a new role by Government as a new interpretation by Government as to what this role should involve. It should be noted that Government measures in pursuance of a positive labour market policy, to increase adaptability and mobility in terms of location, skill and occupation, as exemplified by the Industrial Training Act 1964, and the Redundancy Payments Act 1965, are not by that token a reflection on the competence of trade unions to safeguard the interests of their members so much as a reflection of a determination on the part of Government to make labour market policy the key to economic growth.'

What the TUC memorandum did not mention at this point, however, was the extent to which the trade union Movement—while it may not have taken the initiative in these developments—sharing the general objectives of Government, played an important role in determining the shape of particular legislation. Nor did it mention how trade unionists were actively involved in the machinery set up to implement such legislation. Because, understandably in the circumstances of a Royal Commission investigation, the General Council was over-sensitive to the need to defend the competence of trade unions, it failed to draw the obvious conclusion that had it not been for the trade union Movement much of what is described as the 'complementary' role of the state would not exist in the form that it did: the 'formal indifference' of the state would have again benefited the employers. On the other hand, while recognizing that significant changes were occurring in the role of the state, the TUC General Council was more concerned in its memorandum to defend what it saw as the 'voluntary methods' than it was to adopt a positive attitude of forcing the 'new interpretation' of the role of the state in a direction which would be of benefit to trade unionists. As a result it adopted an indecisive, if not contradictory, stance.

This uncomfortable posture prevails in the trade union Movement's attitude towards the use of legislation as the central feature in a policy to eliminate low pay. In recent years the possibility of using legislation has continually flitted through the discussions on low pay but invariably as a subsidiary or supportive element to the 'voluntary methods', something to be used as a backstop rather than as the main driving force. Yet there is a distinct undercurrent of feeling that sooner or later—as in the case of equal pay—statutory powers will have to be invoked if there is to be any real progress in the campaign against low pay. But, again as in the case of equal pay, there is the danger that this point will not be reached as the result of a conscious decision based on a study of objective factors but as the result of a long slow drift as the 'voluntary methods' fail to deliver the goods.

The main trade union argument, as evidenced by the TUC discussion document, against a legal minimum wage is that by seeking such a statutory minimum the trade union Movement would have no prior assurance that the state would introduce or maintain that minimum at a level acceptable to the unions. This argument is valid only if it is assumed that the Government, or some form of 'independent' body set up by the Government, has the authority to fix the level of the national minimum wage. In nearly all of the discussions on a national minimum wage in Britain this assumption has been made; indeed, it is usually taken for granted. This again demonstrates the weakness of an empirical approach because it simply seeks to take the experience of those countries overseas where a national minimum operates, or the Wages Council machinery in Britain, and to transfer that experience to a national statutory minimum wage applied to Britain. Such an approach is certain to produce an answer which we, along with most other trade unionists, would find unacceptable. This, however, does not invalidate the use of a statutory minimum; only the manner in which it is approached. The correct approach is to pose the problem in another fashion: How can a statutory minimum wage be established and maintained at a level which is acceptable to the trade union Movement? The answer, quite simply, is to consider it as an essential part of the collective bargaining process instead of something which, to use the TUC's phrase, is 'complementary' to it. In other words, instead of leaving it to Government, or some Government-inspired agency, to fix the level of the statutory minimum a system must be developed in which the trade unions have a continuing and direct involvement in determining the level of that minimum.

The outlines of such a system are not difficult to envisage. Each year representatives of the TUC, the CBI and Government would meet and, in a bargaining situation, would reach agreement on the level of the national minimum wage for the next twelve months. That agreement having been reached it would become a statutory obligation on all employers to pay not less than the minimum wage. Industrial Tribunals with suitably extended powers would hear cases, and apply appropriate sanctions, where employers failed to fulfil that obligation.

Such a system has the outstanding merit that it involves the trade union Movement in a positive fashion, whether bargaining on the minimum at national level or taking action through Industrial Tribunals against non-conforming employers at local level. However, as with many systems which are simplicity in outline, it contains profound consequenes for the trade union Movement; consequences which, in our view, can only help to strengthen the Movement in its ability to operate in other fields in addition to wage determination.

One of the weaknesses of the British trade union Movement at the moment is its lack of power at the centre. Although there have been significant developments in this direction in recent years and equally important, increasing recognition by some unions of the need for further developments, the power of the TUC is still relatively small when set against the potential power which could be realized if the collective strength of the nearly ten million workers in TUC affiliated unions were co-ordinated in a centralized fashion. The urgent need is to redefine the relationships between the TUC and its affiliated unions so that individual unions retain their autonomy to act in the areas involving their direct membership interests while the TUC has the authority to act, by co-ordinating the power of affiliated unions, to establish minimum levels on matters of common interest to all unions. Shorter hours and longer holidays are two examples of subjects where, in the past, it has been argued that the TUC could have played a much bigger role and secured much quicker results than were achieved by individual unions bargaining in series of separate negotiations. A national minimum wage, secured by the methods we suggest, would demand that the TUC play such a central role and that, in turn, affiliated unions should not only support the TUC in that role but be actively involved in it.

For example, if the TUC is to be engaged in what is clearly a wage negotiating situation with the CBI and Government the crucial question will be: Where is the TUC's point of reference, how does it decide what is the 'acceptable' level of the national minimum wage? At the moment the TUC General Council has its own definition of what constitutes the minimum wage for a normal week and this is established in a number of ways, partly by arguments set out in the annual Economic Review and partly by resolutions submitted to the annual Congress by individual unions. In the present circumstances this may be an effective method of establishing some kind of target to use in discussions with Government and for individual unions to use in their separate negotiations with employers; but, to put not too fine a point on it, the method is far too primitive to be used in a detailed negotiating situation of the kind that would arise in determining an acceptable national minimum wage. The General Council's annual Economic Review is one of the positive developments of recent years and one which has proved of value to some individual unions in helping to determine their wages strategy. In the context of a national minimum wage it would become a much more important factor because it would be necessary for the General Council to use its assessment of the economic situation in the Economic Review to justify what it considered to be the level of the national minimum wage, expressed as an hourly rate, which it should seek to establish in that year's negotiations with Government and the CBI. Affiliated unions would then be required to study the Review in the light of their own situations and assessments and, if need be, to submit counter-propositions and to debate them with the General Council and the other affiliated unions in the time-honoured fashion. The end result would be the production of a negotiating target to be pursued by the TUC on the authority of its affiliated unions and with their commitment to it through the democratic process.

Such a method, while giving real power to the TUC, would involve a high degree of participation by individual unions and this would effectively counteract any tendencies for the General Council to become divorced from real feelings in the Movement. At the same time, each individual union would have a subjective interest in securing the establishment of a realistic national minimum rate because all subsequent sectional negotiations would, to one degree or another, involve that national minimum as a reference point. Differentials and relativities—whether between or within industries—labour market requirements, relationships between overtime and PBR earnings and basic hourly rates: all of these would need to be placed alongside the national minimum rate when negotiations at the normal industry, company or plant level took place All unions would therefore have two levels of involvement in the negotiating process; one when establishing the national minimum rate through the TUC and the second in the normal bargaining process direct with the employers of members of the union. The only constraint upon a union would be its inability to make a settlement below the statutory national minimum.

Structured in this fashion, the method of establishing the national minimum rate would fit into a pattern of collective bargaining which would be easily recognizable and accepted as such by trade unionists, despite the fact that at the end of the line it relied on statutory enforcement. A further advantage would be that the two levels of involvement would be complementary. Just as the level of the national minimum rate would be a consideration in subsequent sectional negotiations, so the improvements secured over and above the national minimum in those negotiations would become factors which would feature in the Economic Review of the following year and so influence the level of the national minimum sought by the TUC in that year. In this way the trade union Movement would begin to act as a Movement and evolve a total wage strategy which would benefit all workers, not just the lower paid.

So far the assumption has been made that once the claim for a particular level of national minimum has been decided within the trade union Movement the TUC will process that claim and reach a settlement with the Government and the CBI. The possibility must be faced, however, that at some time or another the TUC would find it impossible to reach a settlement on any terms acceptable to the trade unions. What then? This, of course, marks off a fundamental difference between a statutory national minimum wage which is determined in a more or less arbitrary fashion by Government or a Government agency and one which involves the trade union Movement in bargaining. Just as any real collective bargaining situation in the final analysis rests on the ability of the unions to apply sanctions—to strike—so, too, must negotiations on a statutory national minimum rest on that sanction. Given the involvement of the individual unions in the process, and the extent to which the success of their later sectional negotiations will depend on the agreement reached on the national minimum, they must be prepared to authorize the use of the ultimate sanction if the necessity arises. In the reality of such a situation, the failure of the TUC to reach any agreement on a national minimum acceptable to the unions assumes that after all of the concessions, compromises, counter-offers and other procedures that make up negotiations have been exhausted the sum on offer is so far from what is acceptable to the unions that conflict is virtually inevitable. This being the case it would be an early indication that, for one reason or another, the whole wage bargaining scene in that year was likely to be marked by conflict; and that even if the TUC and the unions pruned their demands on the national minimum and eventually accepted what was on offer it would be extremely difficult for individual unions in subsequent sectional negotiations to secure much above the national minimum. The alternative before the trade union Movement in such a situation would be whether to have a total confrontation, which would be likely to be of short duration although extensive in application, in order to win an acceptable national minimum or whether to sell itself short and accept a low national minimum only for individual unions to find themselves at a later stage involved in lengthy and costly disputes in sectional negotiations in an effort to gain small improvements on the national minimum. Confronted with such a choice any realistic trade unionist would probably opt for the first course of action, but the advantage of the system is that it would present the trade union Movement as a whole with the choice and the opportunity to debate and decide in a collective fashion on which alternative course of action to take in the light of the circumstances prevailing at any particular time.

The establishment and maintenance of a statutory minimum wage in the way which we propose therefore not only overcomes the problem that the Government could use it to impose negative wage restraint, it also produces a bonus in that it creates an opportunity for the trade union Movement to maximize its strength in pursuit of common objectives which eventually could be extended beyond the establishment of a national minimum wage to cover minimum standards in other areas, such as hours, holidays and—a matter of growing concern—occupational pensions. Far from limiting the role of trade unionism, this would expand it in a very real fashion in a way which would not involve the risk of corporate statism.

Just as this system would not limit the role of trade unionism so it would not inhibit the development of trade union organization amongst the low paid, which is another argument used against the statutory minimum wage. The need to constantly police the annually changing minimum rate at local level, and to institute proceedings against offending employers through the Industrial Dispute Tribunals, would open up major possibilities for union organization and recruitment amongst the lower paid. So, too, would the need for effective trade unionism to undertake the functions of promoting and monitoring efficiency and development in the low paid industries as outlined in Chapter 6. Finally, the national minimum rate would not replace sectional negotiations in any industry—whether high paid or low paid. It would still be a function for unions to negotiate in the traditional low paid industries and occupations to secure improvements above the national minimum and to establish the relationship between the various components of total earnings, such as overtime and PBR payments, which produced the most beneficial combination of hours and earnings.

We have shown that there is no principle or practical reason why the trade union Movement should not initiate a campaign against low pay embracing a statutory minimum wage structured in the way we have suggested. Fears that it will enhance the role of the state and diminish the role of the trade unions, or that it will inhibit trade union organizations, are without foundation. Indeed, if the trade union Movement takes the initiative in the way we suggest it will not only act against low pay, it will do so in a way which will immeasurably strengthen the power of the organized working class.

The solution to the problem of low pay must come through political action and, for socialists, political action can never be merely a matter of electoral organization to secure a majority in Parliament. Nor can it be considered, as is sometimes suggested, just a matter of power. More precisely it is a matter of the establishment and application of power: what counts is on the basis of what objectives electoral supremacy is secured and what subsequent use is made of the effective strength of Government in alliance with the Labour Movement to realize those objectives. If the Labour Party is to sustain itself as a political force and to justify its separate existence it must continually demonstrate that it is prepared to use political power in a different fashion and to realize different objectives than the parties of the Right and Centre, the Tories and the Liberals. It was the failure of the Labour Party in the 'fifties and the 'sixties to adopt policies which would have enabled it to make such a distinction which rendered it incapable of attacking low pay as one of the major economic manifestations of the inequalities of a competitive and acquisitive society.

The attitude of mind which permeated the Labour Party during that period can best be described as one which led to an ideological coalition with the Tories and, while reflected in the posture of many Party leaders, was perhaps most strikingly illustrated by Herbert Morrison in his autobiography[5] published in 1960, a year after the Labour Party in which he had played a prominent role in policy formation had experienced its third successive general election defeat. Looking back on the post-war years, Morrison commented that, 'irrespective of political factors', the 1945 general election had been a landmark in British social and economic history because since then all parties had fought general elections on the basis of their own versions of *Let Us Face The Future*—Labour's 1945 election programme. He said that the policy makers of all parties had accepted, in some measure, what the Labour Party in 1945 had been 'fortunate or intelligent enough to recognize first.' What was this startling discovery which had changed the character of British politics? That 'irrespective of class, age or occupation' the modern British adult had a thoughtful and responsible attitude. In other words, Morrison was advancing the common argument that class considerations were no longer an important factor in determining party allegiances.

This attitude was reinforced by other views expressed by Morrison in his autobiography. Preoccupied, as were many of his colleagues at that time, with the impact of the alleged affluent society on the Labour Movement, he discovered what he descibed as the 'new working class' which owned washing machines and television sets, and he pointed to the fact that 'a considerable number of working class men and women now pay income tax—once the hallmark of middle and upper class standards.' From this it was an easy step for him to conclude that 'a number of the working class are beginning to regard themselves as middle class'; and he speculated on what can be regarded as both a complementary and contradictory question: whether sections of the Tory Party might 'become restless at Macmillan's steady attempts to appear to out-socialize the Socialists.'

It must be remembered that at the time Morrison and others were expressing these views the Ministry of Labour distribution of earnings survey and other studies were demonstrating that behind the plastic facade of the affluent society many working class families were struggling to make ends meet on poverty line wages. Vic Allen, in his book *Trade Unions and Government*,[6] which was published in the same year as Morrison's autobiography, observed that 'a Labour Party which is exhausting its social inspiration and an adaptable Conservative Party can be remarkably similar'. He summarized the views, if not the language, of many low paid workers in that period.

It would be impossible for the Labour Party even to contemplate an effective attack on low pay while at the same time adhering to the belief that it must dilute its general political philosophy in order to present itself as a classless party. An understanding of the inconsistency involved in such a stance was shown by Aneurin Bevan, when he said that poverty, great wealth and democracy were ultimately incompatible elements. The function of parliamentary democracy, he asserted, was to expose wealth and privilege to the attack of the people: 'It is a sword pointed at the heart of property power.'[7]

It is in such a context that a policy to eliminate low pay, based on a statutory minimum wage and embracing a wide range of parallel measures designed to end the economic and social circumstances which create and perpetuate low pay, must be considered by the Labour Party and its natural ally the trade union Movement. For, as Professor Tawney[8] once so aptly commented, democracy is not only a form of government but a type of society which requires the conversion of economic power into the servant of society and the resolute elimination of all forms of special privilege which favour some groups and depress others.

Low pay is not an irritating pimple or a minor blemish on the unacceptable face of capitalism, which can be eased by a soothing ointment or discreetly hidden by a suitable cosmetic. It is a basic feature of the bone structure which contributes to the total unacceptability of that face. If the Labour Movement is to be serious in its intent to eliminate low pay it must act as a surgeon rather than a first aid attendant.

Notes

Chapter 2: THE AFFLUENT SOCIETY

1. Source: *Ministry of Labour Gazette*, April 1961.
2. Source: *Ministry of Labour Gazette*, June 1961.
3. Robinson, D. 'Low Paid Workers and Incomes Policy', *Bulletin of the Oxford University Institute of Economics and Statistics*, Vol. 29, No. 1, pp. 1–29 (February 1967).
4. Marquand, J. 'Which Are The Lowest Paid Workers?' *British Journal of Industrial Relations*, Vol. 5, pp. 359–374, (1967).
5. B. Abel-Smith and P. Townsend, 'The Poor and the Poorest', *Occasional Papers in Social Administration No. 17*, Bell, 1965.
6. *Circumstances of Families*, HMSO, July 1967.
7. *Administration of the Wage Stop*, HMSO, December 1967.

Chapter 3: AN OPPORTUNITY MISSED

1. TUC Report 1963.
2. Labour Party Annual Conference Report 1963.
3. *Productivity, Prices and Incomes*, Report of a Conference of Executive Committees of Affiliated Organizations, TUC, April 1965.
4. Report of 44th National Conference, NUPE, 1965.
5. TUC Report 1965.
6. TUC Report 1966.
7. *Incomes Policy*, Report of a Conference of Executive Committees of Affiliated Organizations, TUC, March 1967.
8. *Price and Incomes Standstill: Period of Severe Restraint*, HMSO, 1966.
9. *The Pay and Conditions of Manual Workers in Local Authorities, the National Health Service, Gas and Water Supply*, HMSO, 1967.
10. Alan Fels, *The British Prices and Incomes Board*, Cambridge University Press, 1972.
11. TUC Report 1967.
12. *Economic Review and Report of a Conference of Executive Committees of Affiliated Organizations*, TUC, 1968.

13. Economic Review 1969, TUC.
14. *A National Minimum Wage*, Report of an Inter-Departmental Working Party, HMSO, 1969.
15. *Low Pay:* TUC General Council Discussion Document, TUC, 1970.
16. TUC Report 1970.
17. NBPI, Report No. 169, *General Problems of Low Pay*, HMSO, 1971.

Chapter 4: THE POLITICS RESTATED

1. *A Programme for Controlling Inflation: The First Stage*, HMSO, 1972.
2. *Economic Policy and Collective Bargaining in 1973*, Report to a Special Trades Union Congress, TUC, 1973.
3. Pay Board, Advisory Report 2, *Relativities*, HMSO, 1974.
4. Labour Party Annual Conference Report 1973.

Chapter 5: MEANS AND ENDS

1. *A Special Case? Social Justice and the Miners*, Edited for the NUM by John Hughes and Roy Moore, Penguin Books, 1972.
2. *Prices and Incomes Standstill: Period of Severe Restraint*, HMSO, 1966.
3. *A National Minimum Wage*, Report of an Inter-Departmental Working Party, HMSO, 1969.
4. NBPI, Report No. 169, *General Problems of Low Pay*, HMSO, 1971.
5. Hansard, Vol. 780, No. 86, Col. 1625, 26 March 1969.
6. D.H.S.S. Press Release, No. 70/100, 17 April 1970.
7. Rhodes Boyson (ed.), *Down With the Poor*, Churchill Press Ltd, 1971.

Chapter 7: THE NUMBERS GAME

1. All of the statistical material in this, and the following Chapter, is derived from the results of the 1973 *New Earnings Survey* published in the Department of Employment Gazette, October, November, December, 1973.
2. This study could be extended by examining all industries under Minimum List Headings. We refrained from this because (i) much of the information is not published for each MLH industry, (ii) such a study would have added length and detail out of character with a book intended for active trade unionists rather than economists or statisticians, and (iii) the general argument emerges clearly from our limited study of the SIC industries.

Chapter 9: THE GRAND ALLIANCE

1. *The History of the TUC 1868–1968, A Pictorial Survey of a Social Revolution*, TUC, 1968.

2. *Trade Unionism : The Evidence of the Trades Union Congress to the Royal Commission on Trade Unions and Employers' Associations*, TUC, 1966.
3. TUC Report 1945.
4. *Low Pay*, TUC General Discussion Document, TUC, 1970.
5. Lord Morrison, *Herbert Morrison An Autobiography*, Odhams Press, 1960.
6. V. Allen, *Trade Unions and Government*, Longmans, 1960.
7. A. Bevan, *In Place of Fear*, Heinemann, 1952.
8. R. H. Tawney, *Equality*, Allen & Unwin, 1952.